CHANGING THE SUBJECT

CHANGING THE SUBJECT

A Theory of Rhetorical Empathy

LISA BLANKENSHIP

UTAH STATE UNIVERSITY PRESS
Logan

© 2019 by University Press of Colorado

Published by Utah State University Press
An imprint of University Press of Colorado
245 Century Circle, Suite 202
Louisville, Colorado 80027

 The University Press of Colorado is a proud member of
the Association of University Presses.

The University Press of Colorado is a cooperative publishing enterprise sup-
ported, in part, by Adams State University, Colorado State University, Fort
Lewis College, Metropolitan State University of Denver, Regis University,
University of Colorado, University of Northern Colorado, University of
Wyoming, Utah State University, and Western Colorado University.

∞ This paper meets the requirements of the ANSI/NISO Z39.48–1992
(Permanence of Paper)

ISBN: 978-1-60732-909-1 (paperback)
ISBN: 978-1-60732-910-7 (ebook)
https://doi.org/10.7330/9781607329107

Library of Congress Cataloging-in-Publication Data

Names: Blankenship, Lisa, 1970– author.
Title: Changing the subject : a theory of rhetorical empathy / Lisa
  Blankenship.
Description: Logan : Utah State University Press, [2018] | Includes bibliograph-
  ical references and index.
Identifiers: LCCN 2019020509 | ISBN 9781607329091 (pbk.) | ISBN
  9781607329107 (ebook)
Subjects: LCSH: Rhetoric. | Empathy.
Classification: LCC P301 .B55 2018 | DDC 808—dc23
LC record available at https://lccn.loc.gov/2019020509

The University Press of Colorado gratefully acknowledges the generous support of the City University of New York toward the publication of this book.

Cover illustration © Derek Brumby/Shutterstock.com

To my father, Larry Blankenship,
who, for me, has always embodied rhetorical empathy.

CONTENTS

ACKNOWLEDGMENTS

Thanks to so many for making this book much better than it would have been otherwise. It would not have *been* otherwise.

To the writers whose stories I share in these pages, and whose activism and hope have inspired me: Joyce Fernandes, Justin Lee, Rachel Held Evans, Kathy Baldock, and my students at Baruch College, City University of New York.

To my colleagues and writing-group partners in the faculty fellowship publication program at CUNY: Rosanne Carlo, Olivia Moy, Jorge Matos, Jennifer Maloy, Simon Reader, and especially our esteemed leader, Carrie Hintz, who encouraged me from the beginning to "write beautiful sentences." I'm grateful to the Weissman School of Arts and Sciences at Baruch College for a semester of leave from my writing program director responsibilities to help get this book off the ground. I'm also grateful to my colleagues at Baruch, who have been incredibly supportive since I arrived in New York four years ago: Eva Chou for supporting me in more ways than one in this process; Mary McGlynn for keeping it all together; Shelly Eversley for her leadership in the FFPP and her friendship since day one; Gerry Dalgish for his mentorship and good humor; Tim Aubry and John Brenkman for valuable insights on the work in progress; and Cheryl Smith for believing in me and sticking things out and for inviting me into her community of writers and friends. Thanks to her, Maria Jerskey, and Leigh Jones for insights on the early stages of this book and for helping me believe I could finish. Thanks also to Amy Wan for moral support and friendship.

Thanks to my Montclair State community: Lee Behlman and Emily Isaacs, for reading and feedback and for persuading me finally to let go of the manuscript. To Jessica Restaino, for Fridays in the Montclair Public Library with our headphones on, writing, and for making this long journey much more rewarding.

Thanks also to Paula Mathieu for generous support, to Eric Leake for his work on empathy in a parallel universe, and to Seth Graves for his provocative thoughts on the ideas in this book.

To my Miami University colleagues and friends: Madelyn Detloff, Jason Palmeri, LuMing Mao, Cindy Lewiecki-Wilson, Heidi McKee, the late David Cowan, a gentle, beautiful soul, Ann Updike, Dominic Ashby, Scott Wagar, and the inimitable Kate Ronald, whose work on pragmatism and women's rhetorics inspired this project and a generation of scholars now scattered across the country, and whose friendship sustained me through hard waters. I owe a great debt also to Travis Webster for reading the nearly final manuscript and offering valuable feedback and encouragement.

The Coalition of Feminist Scholars in the History of Rhetoric and Composition has long been a source of caring solidarity. I'm grateful also to have been part of the Kenneth Burke seminar at the Rhetoric Society of America Summer Institute at the University of Wisconsin–Madison in June 2015 and to have benefitted from its smart, generous participants from across the United States and abroad.

I'm grateful to the reviewers of the manuscript for Utah State University Press and especially to Rachael Levay, who believed in this project and whose editorial questions helped me imagine a broader audience. I also owe a tremendous debt of gratitude to Kami Day, copyeditor extraordinaire and one of my aspirational humans.

I'm fortunate to have met Michele Eodice years ago through the University of Oklahoma Writing Center. Her mentorship and friendship over the years have been incredibly meaningful to me, and her insights and good advice helped make this project a reality.

This book has been a labor of love in more ways than one. I'm thankful for my parents, Larry and Beverly, for making this and many other things possible. For my brother Craig for his humor and unwavering support. For Genevieve, always, who helped me see the world, and the Other, in new ways.

Finally, to Caroline—for laughter, and for loving me back to life. I can't imagine any of this without you.

CHANGING THE SUBJECT

Introduction
CHANGING THE SUBJECT

From the place where we are right
flowers will never grow
in the spring.
The place where we are right
is hard and trampled
like a yard.
But doubts and loves
dig up the world
like a mole, a plough.
And a whisper will be heard in the place
where the ruined
house once stood.
— Yehuda Amichai, "The Place
Where We Are Right"

On a sweltering summer day in 1963, civil rights leader Medgar Evers was gunned down in his driveway in Jackson, Mississippi. That same night, lifelong Jackson native Eudora Welty wrote a fictional account of the shooting from the perspective of the killer. It was published less than a month later in the *New Yorker*, the two pages of prose so realistic many believed it was written by the killer himself.[1] In an interview in 1972, she talked about writing the story and her understanding of the killer's motivations.

> That night I thought to myself, I've lived here all of my life. I know the kind of mind that did this. This was before anyone was caught. So I wrote a story in the first person as the murderer because I thought, I'm in a position where I know. I know what this man must feel like. I've lived with this kind of thing. . . . What I was writing about was that world of hate I felt I had grown up with and I felt I could speak as someone who knew it. I wrote from deep feeling and horror.[2]

In "Must the Novelist Crusade?," she writes that "a plot is a thousand times more unsettling than an argument."[3] While the best

DOI: 10.7330/9781607329107.c000

fiction avoids directly moralizing or persuading, stories—and the pathos they arouse—are the great bridge between literary and rhetorical discourse, between Aristotle's foundational treatises on poetics and rhetoric. The act of writing stories, whether fiction or nonfiction, consists largely in trying to inhabit the world, both interior and exterior, of an Other, an act of imagination that has led scholars of literary theory to pursue the question of whether reading others' stories makes us more empathetic, more sensitive, more able to listen and understand.[4] During a conversation between President Barack Obama and novelist Marilynne Robison in 2015, Obama told his own story about the relationship of reading others' stories and the cultivation of empathy.

> When I think about how I understand my role as citizen, setting aside being president, and the most important set of understandings that I bring to that position of citizen, the most important stuff I've learned I think I've learned from novels. It has to do with empathy. It has to do with being comfortable with the notion that the world is complicated and full of grays, but there's still truth there to be found, and that you have to strive for that and work for that. And the notion that it's possible to connect with some[one] else even though they're very different from you.[5]

As painful as it can be in our present moment to be reminded of national leaders with an empathetic philosophy formed by taking seriously the stories—real and imagined—of those very different from us, it's important to stay focused, both in times of peril and otherwise, on the role of empathy and connecting across difference.

How we make these connections is of vital interest politically as well as morally. As educators, as scholars of rhetorical theory informed by postmodern critiques of inequality and by feminist theories dedicated to pointing out historical and contemporary injustices and amplifying the voices speaking out against them, we are highly invested in developing theories that offer ways of forging alliances across differences. In our age of tremendous polarization between right and left, black and white, rural and urban, us and them, the need for ways of connecting across difference could not be more urgent. This book, the first sustained exploration of empathy in rhetorical theory, examines how writers in public, digital, and transnational locations ethically engage with one another across pronounced differences. What do these engagements across difference have in common? How can we (further) develop such practices and habits of mind in ourselves and in our students?

This book's premise is that pathos—appeals to the personal in the form of stories and the (always political) emotions that can ensue—is one of the most powerful forms of persuasion and change. My purpose is to frame pathos in new ways and make a case for *rhetorical empathy* as a means of ethical rhetorical engagement. I define rhetorical empathy as both a topos and a trope, a choice and habit of mind that invents and invites discourse informed by deep listening and its resulting emotion, characterized by narratives based on personal experience.[6] Rhetorical empathy is both a hermeneutic and a heuristic, a way of thinking (and feeling) constituted by language and a way of using language.

Empathy can be a slippery term. Why am I using that concept in particular, with so much cultural baggage, especially for women, and why use it in the context of engaging across difference? I discuss the similarities among sympathy, pity, compassion, and empathy and what the similarities mean for a study of rhetorical empathy in chapter 1, "A Brief History of Empathy," by tracing threads of empathy and similar concepts through rhetorical history, in the Greco-Roman tradition and beyond. I choose *empathy* rather than its various similar alternatives for a number of reasons. *Pity* and *sympathy* are even more culturally loaded terms than empathy in their associations with patronization, colonization, and a somewhat removed experience of an Other's plight. From its beginning, empathy has signified an immersion in an Other's experience through verbal and visual artistic expression. This element of an immersive experience that results in an emotional response, as well as the associations of empathy with altruism and social justice, possibly explains its continued linguistic cachet over terms such as *pity* and *sympathy*.[7] In my definition of empathy, I focus on the topoi of empathy in terms of how the subject positions themself in relation to the object. Rhetorical empathy becomes both a *place* and a *stance*. I situate rhetorical empathy as coming alongside or feeling *with* the experiences of an Other rather than feeling *for* or displacing an Other, which is usually associated with pity or sympathy.

For every piece of scholarship on empathy in English in the last century—most of it within psychology and philosophy—there seems to be a different signification for empathy: "a cognitive process analogous to cognitive role taking or perspective taking"; "a primarily affective process (having some cognitive components)"; "an affective response more appropriate to someone else's situation than to one's own"; "other-oriented feelings of concern, compassion, and tenderness experienced as a result of witnessing another person's suffering"; "sharing the perceived emotion of another—'feeling with' another."[8] As Lauren Wispé notes, the "trails back" to the original rhetorical contexts and struggles over definitions have become "overgrown with redefinitions [and] reinterpretations."[9] Kristie Fleckenstein points out that "sympathy, pity, compassion, empathy are slippery terms made even more slippery as usage shifts within and between disciplines."[10]

In Euro-American epistemology, specifically within psychology, empathy often is associated with either cognition/thought or affect/emotion: *cognitive empathy* and *affective empathy*.[11] Rhetorical empathy functions as a conscious choice to connect with an Other—an inventional topos and a rhetorical strategy or *pisteis*—that can result in an emotional response. It is difficult to parse out the distinction between thought and emotion or, in other words, empathy, as a deliberate, cognitive function or a subconscious response we might associate with emotion. Work in cultural studies (Ahmed), rhetorical theory (Gross), and neuroscience (Decety and Meyer) has complicated the degree to which emotions (including empathy) are considered hard-wired components of our biological makeup or cognitive functions highly dependent on context and learned behavior.

This book is not meant be an exhaustive study of the concept of empathy. It is an exploration of what happens when we think about *rhetoric* and *empathy* together. In joining these two incredibly complicated terms, my intention is not to create an oxymoron, as if by association with the popular concept of rhetoric, empathy becomes strategic to the point that it is entirely performative, although there certainly is a deliberate, performative aspect to rhetorical empathy. Neither do I want to take away from the strategic and social aspects of rhetoric by placing it with the term *empathy*, as if empathy is something located solely in the individual, an emotional connection unrelated to social codes and beliefs constructed, circulated, and maintained through language systems.

By combining the two, my intention is to highlight aspects of each: *rhetoric* as a strategic use of symbol systems using various modes of communication—language, still and moving images, and sound. And *empathy* as both a conscious, deliberate attempt to understand an Other *and* the emotions that can result from such attempts—often subconscious, though culturally influenced.[12] Empathy, like rhetoric, is an epistemology, a way of knowing and understanding, a complex combination of intention and emotion. While empathy in some respects has become almost clichéd, signifying for some a way of reinscribing existing power relations under the guise of sympathetic identification, rhetorical empathy can shift power dynamics among interlocutors by means of the very connections that may on the surface seem like conservatizing reifications. Empathy is never simple; its complexities make it one of the most difficult rhetorical topoi to think with and enact.

Julie Lindquist touches on the complex relationship between a conscious, deliberate, and strategic use of empathy and the often-unconscious responses emotions can create in us. In her article "Class Affects, Classroom Affectations: Working through the Paradoxes of Strategic Empathy," she uses an example of her own explorations of assuming what she calls "strategic empathy" in a first-year writing course focused on working-class rhetoric and informed by critical pedagogy. She describes her dilemma of being in a position of power as the instructor yet wanting to approach her students fairly and without simply imposing her own views. Building on the work of Hephzibah Roskelly and Kate Ronald's romantic/pragmatic rhetoric, she argues that the work of such a course—and our pedagogy regardless of our theoretical influences—should take into account the very real effects theories have within the classroom. She describes a scenario that happened in the course in which she "performed empathy" and what happened as a result.

She analyzes her performance with her students and their responses using the concepts surface acting and deep acting, based on the work of sociologist Laura Grindstaff and her appropriation of Arlie Hochschild's *The Managed Heart: Commercialization of Human Feeling*. Both types of acting are deliberately assumed, affective displays. In surface acting, Lindquist explains, "You remain in control of your emotions by consciously structuring the impressions you produce," and in deep acting, "you relinquish the possibility of emotional control."[13] Surface acting can come across as disingenuous: seeming to be empathetic rather than actually becoming empathetic. Deep acting happens when someone isn't trying to seem happy or sad but these emotions occur spontaneously as a result of surface acting, "a real feeling that has been self-induced."[14] Deep acting involves, then, an emotional component that cannot be faked or controlled—entirely. Both surface acting and deep acting involve on a certain level a purposeful choice to display emotion, but deep acting includes an element of change within the rhetor: "When you deep act, in other words, you work, through acts of will and imagination, to open yourself to the possibility that you might *persuade yourself* that the emotions you are presenting are real. You risk *becoming* the thing you are performing. Deep acting is, paradoxically, the process of exerting control in order to relinquish control."[15]

Lindquist compares deep acting to the writing process: experiencing it is the goal of empathetic rhetoric, "but one moves toward it through the rhetorical work of surface acting."[16] This description of how rhetorical emotions function is, in many respects, a fake-it-'til-you-make-it approach. An empathetic approach may not be deeply ingrained, but through habit and attempting to approach a rhetorical situation and an Other empathetically, effects of the sort she associates with deep acting can occur: we're changed in the process. Strategic empathy becomes a rhetoric that is "simultaneously empathetic and critical," a deliberate attempt to resist what Lindquist calls "postmodern paralysis."[17]

She describes the scenario in the course in which these concepts played out. The Iraq War had just started, and she felt it was odd in the context of their class discussions to not bring up what was then the elephant in the room. She writes that neither of the two former approaches she had taken in such cases, "neutrality (taking no position) or 'honesty' (communicating my real feelings about the ethics of the war directly)" had worked very well, so she decided she needed "another way to be with students, one that would enable the emotional responses that discussion of this issue was likely to invite."[18] She became vulnerable. She decided to learn from them what they wanted and needed from her.

> I told them that, given our very different positions on the war (they were generally pro, I was fervently con) and my position of relative power over them, I was having trouble imagining how to negotiate the discussion responsibility. I asked them to consider a scenario in which they were teachers in precisely my situation, teachers trying to figure out how to respond ethically and productively to a political issue about which they had strong feelings—keeping in mind that they (as teachers) had the power to silence students whose views were different from theirs.[19]

They responded that if they were in her shoes, they would share their own view but as one of many possibilities. The result was that she created an atmosphere of trust in which they felt they could share their stories and views without being judged, yet they knew where she stood as well. In hearing their stories, the *why* behind them began to emerge for her; in other words, their motivations began to be clearer to her and they became real people. In *staging empathy*—performing empathy even though

at the initial stages she was highly resistant to their views—she
began to move toward *deep empathy*. She writes that

> what made this strategy work, I think, was my willingness to
> make myself strategically naïve in two moments: first, in seeking
> advice about *how* we should conduct discussions about the war,
> and then later, when (working hard against my own emotional
> need to negatively evaluate some of the perspectives I was hear-
> ing about the war) I worked to communicate empathy for their
> positions as *affective responses*.[20]

Affect is wrapped up in cultural discourses and ideologies,
not (just) an individual response. Yet in hearing them relate
their stories (some had friends and partners in the war, some
were from conservative families, etc.), she gained the perspective she needed to see them as individuals and real people—and
as members of larger groups with motivations that clearly
informed and constructed their positions to a large degree. In
performing empathy toward them, and in asking them to do so
in return to some degree, she began to have deep empathy for
them as people, even though they continued to disagree about
the Iraq War and war in general.

Her account draws attention to the relationship among our
emotional responses, our social discourses, our (emotional)
connections or disconnections to an Other and their motivations, and our will. Emotions and empathy are rhetorical.
Whether functioning on a deliberate, strategic, conscious level
or on an affective level influenced by experience—and rhetorical empathy involves both—empathy is encompassed, created,
and expressed within and through language and cultural codes.

Depending on your vantage point, the idea of empathy as a
way of engaging with difference can be read as overly ambitious,
naïve, or simply common sense. After spending the past several
years studying how people are able to connect with one another
across profound difference, I offer this conclusion: approaching
others in rhetorical engagements must begin with changing ourselves, with listening, with trying to understand the personal and
political factors that influence the person who makes our blood
boil. This approach to rhetoric is very different from one that

listens to others in order to make a point and to change them. It goes beyond audience analysis and considering our audience and instead asks that we become vulnerable enough to consider our own motives, our blind spots, and our prejudice. Adopting this stance is vital for people with privilege; it is no longer an option. I write this as a queer, white professor with working-class roots who considers it no longer an option for myself. An approach based on rhetorical empathy can help those with little power and privilege sustain efforts to fight the status quo and to maintain perspective. An effort to listen to and understand others, especially those very different from us, helps us be better humans and more able to react in ethical and rhetorically effective ways. Ultimately, it helps sustain us in the midst of polarization and, in some cases, deep and traumatic injustice.

Engaging in what I call *rhetorical empathy* is hard work, but it's important, and some would argue it's the foundation of our work as educators. In this book, I include case studies that demonstrate various aspects of rhetorical empathy across a variety of marked social differences, including social class, race, and the intersections of gender, sexuality, and religion. I focus on the rhetoric of two labor activists—a Jane Addams speech in late nineteenth-century Gilded Age Chicago and the social media stories of Joyce Fernandes in Brazil; the online rhetoric of gay-rights activist Justin Lee; and the use of stories in public arguments by students in my classes at Baruch College at the City University of New York.

ORIGIN STORIES

This work is informed by pragmatism's emphasis on the material consequences of our theories and by feminist theories that value praxis.[21] In light of this theoretical basis and my emphasis on how our stories inform our practice and thinking, my own story about how I came to be interested in empathy as a basis for rhetoric forms an important thread in this book. As important as empathy and engaging across difference are in a pluralistic society, I came to this project for highly practical and deeply personal reasons ten years ago. I left my familiar and safe world as a writer and creative director to go to graduate school—a big enough change by itself—but I also fell in love and (finally) began the process of coming out, first to myself after many years of struggling with my sexuality in a conservative, Bible-belt culture in the 1980s and 90s, and then to my family and friends. By far the biggest challenge in my coming-out process was my faith: I was raised in a conservative Christian church, and now I'd complicated my life a great deal by falling in love not only with another woman, but with a woman who'd been involved with queer activism since she'd come out as a teenager. In college she was the leader of a Gay-Straight Alliance group, and she'd lived for a short time in San Francisco and interned for GLAAD (Gay and Lesbian Alliance Against Defamation). On top of this, complicating matters further, she was an atheist. I, on the other hand, was a lifelong Christian with (theologically conservative) clergy on both sides of my family. I had even, for a time, considered entering the ministry and spent a year in seminary after college. In my conservative faith, being (openly) gay was not an option.

She and I told each other our stories in the many hours we spent together. Based on her experiences, she'd formed views of Christians that were, to me, stereotypes. They didn't sound like the Christians I knew. But she also had good reason to not trust Christians when it came to the issue of being gay; she'd been burned too many times to trust them. It shook my world to hear a voice from the other side of a large wall separating "those people" outside my familiar discourse community from the voices inside that formed such a large part of who I was at that time. I soon realized her stories were not that different from my own in certain ways. In other ways we could not have been more different.

We changed each other, but more precisely we each became more vulnerable and honest about ourselves. She had been drawn to faith as a child but had been so turned off by what she saw of organized religion as a teenager and adult that she never gave it a second thought; I had known for twenty years that I was gay, but for the first time I was motivated enough (by love) to risk being wrong and losing other parts of my life, and I took a leap. And was it a leap. I was able, finally, to be honest. It was both exhilarating and terrifying.

I lived for a time in a swirl of emotions, both elation at being able to be honest and despair over losing many people in my life who believed being gay and Christian are incompatible and who couldn't deal with the cognitive dissonance I represented. Here was a person they knew and loved and who wasn't "like those people": troubled queers whose lives were in shambles because they'd run from the truth. It was becoming clearer to me that many of the troubles of queer people were caused at least in part by being rejected by their families and people they love. Instead of listening, asking questions, and trying to understand my journey and walking with me in it, most of the people in my life went into a "don't ask, don't tell" mode. Someone I particularly respected told me on the phone one day that I was the biggest disappointment of her life. Fortunately, I was in my mid-thirties as I listened to these words, tears streaming down my face, and not an eighteen-year-old who was being thrown out of the house and disowned by their family. I had seen this happen more times than I wanted to count. I understand very well why some people never come out.

In the midst of this pain, I still believed firmly that my friends and family who disagreed with my "lifestyle"—and even those who would no longer associate with me—were well-intentioned people who never would consider themselves homophobic or hateful. I struggled a great deal with this dissonance and tried to bridge the widening gap between us. In that process, I realized quickly that using logical arguments would go nowhere ("But the church has been wrong before about so many things: what about slavery, and now divorce is so common and once was taboo?"). I looked for other ways to try to understand what seemed to be an abyss of difference between us, and I also needed a way to allay my own hurt and anger. I was looking for a book like the one I've written.

This study, then, began as a very personal question for me ten years ago when I began graduate school: how were queer people and queer allies who identified as religious navigating the rhetoric of antigay people in their own communities? Much of the rhetoric in the intersection of religion and gay rights is toxic and polarizing, despite the great strides made in acceptance and understanding of LGBTQ people in recent years. I was interested in leaders of progay movements in religious contexts who were making inroads by using a compassionate approach to the very people who had ostracized and demonized them. The fact that people could hold radically different views on such a contentious topic—one so close to my own experience—and manage to find ways of overcoming their differences, or at least continue to talk to one another despite them, fascinated me and developed into this study.

My coming-out experience and growing up in the Bible belt taught me what it means to work for justice for queer people, starting with myself, and at the same time not dismiss people on the conservative side of the political spectrum. Recent events in our country have given me perspective on the need for resistance and protest and also the need for attempting to understand people who would not openly embrace racism, sexism, and homophobia but who nonetheless implicitly endorse them with their apathy and votes.

From the story I just described, I learned that the Other is, in many ways, not so different from me, yet the differences I encountered changed me in profound ways. I also learned the value of listening and being open to being changed rather than (only) trying to reinforce my own identity by persuading others to agree with me. That kind of vulnerability, on some level, changes others, but in the process we ourselves are changed. It was a profound lesson for someone raised in an evangelical Christian culture that values, above all, converting others, and that believes changing one's mind and being open to others are forms of compromise rather than ways of learning and becoming better. The kind of closed-mindedness I had internalized in that culture has felt eerily familiar in the years since as I've watched Tea Party purists in the US Congress shut down the government based on what they view as principle. How can we function as a democracy and as a pluralistic culture when only our way is right—especially if our way is "God's way"? This question is vitally important to our democracy, and my story and the theory I offer in this book hopefully can provide some helpful perspective. I have walked on both sides of a very wide gap, and this book, in a sense, is that story.

How can a peace-based, supremely feminist, antiracist practice such as empathy have any impact in our culture? From an educator's perspective, how do we teach writing and ethical rhetorical engagement in the midst of tremendous polarization? These are the questions driving this project.

CONTRIBUTION TO RHETORICAL THEORY AND WRITING STUDIES

While I don't deny that a primary purpose of rhetoric since Aristotle has been changing others and discerning how we ourselves are being shaped by discourse, this book takes as its goal a shift in the focus of rhetoric itself. If changing others is the goal, a more sustainable approach may be first to change ourselves. Rhetorical praxis based on listening and empathy does not necessarily change systemic conditions or even an immediate interlocutor or audience. It does, however, hold potential for changing the speaker or writer and for shifting the focus from changing an Other to understanding an Other. Such moves are an important contribution of feminist rhetorical theories on which this project relies and which I discuss in chapter 1. In its focus on changing the self versus primarily an Other in rhetorical engagement, rhetorical empathy is closely aligned with reflective practices that have developed and become highly influential in writing studies over the past twenty years in the work of, for example, Donna Qualley and Kathleen Blake Yancey.[22]

A stance based on rhetorical empathy helps writers reach audiences different from themselves by imagining what their audience's motives are. What do people's views (and, more important, the stories behind them) suggest about them as individuals as well as about their place in systemic discourses? Rhetorical empathy results in an emotional engagement that can disarm; it asks for vulnerability from the speaker or writer that can, at times, promote it in return. It is born from a stance (topos) of learning and adjusting rather than first and foremost trying to make a point and change an audience. The results of such a stance are personal narratives and emotional appeals that help writers and rhetors present themselves as real and identifiable rather than as a stereotype.

Rhetorical empathy circulates both ways: it's initiated by the speaker or writer toward an audience and ideally reciprocated by the audience in return, often as a result of the audience's being treated with dignity rather than as a stereotype or with (often justifiable) anger. It's recursive: it cannot happen without a rhetor or writer listening in the first place, reacting or acting toward an Other in a spirit of goodwill rather than anger. This approach can invite the same response in turn rather than defensiveness or stalemate. It changes the subject of discourse—both the content of discourse and its agent, and as a result it holds the potential for bridging difficult rhetorical impasses. When an interlocutor says, for example, "I once held your view, and I didn't think I was being hateful at the time," as gay-rights activist Justin Lee writes to his conservative Christian audience in chapter 3, it can have the effect of diffusing rhetorically loaded words that cause people to shut down rather than listen in return. This kind of approach is not necessarily manipulative; in fact, if it's done with any degree of sincerity, it can have the effect of softening how a rhetor views their audience and can increase the chances that not only will the audience listen but that doors will be open for further engagement, listening, and learning.

CONTEXT AND EXIGENCY

In recent years, researchers have studied empathy from the perspective of cognitive science (Decety and Jackson), psychology (Eisenberg and Strayer, Hoffman), philosophy (Vetlesen), and literary theory (Keen). Scholars in cultural studies (Ahmed, Berlant, Sedgwick) and rhetorical theory (Gross, Micciche) have focused on affect more broadly. Within writing studies, valuable work has focused on empathy in pedagogical contexts (Lindquist, Richmond, DeStigter, Leake), in public discourse and deliberation (Lynch, Fleckenstein), and in relation to Rogerian rhetoric (Teich, Peary).

Dennis Lynch makes the case that while empathy was once the centerpiece of modern rhetoric, it has been critiqued, as I outline in detail in chapter 1, by postmodern rhetorical theories that foreground the body and power struggles.[23] Empathy has been overshadowed in postmodern theories by the "hermeneutics of suspicion" (Ricoeur) and a much-needed focus on difference and power. In her defense of empathy as one of the goals of literary study, Ann Jurecic points to Paul Ricoeur's belief that hermeneutics "seems to be animated by [a] double motivation: [a] willingness to suspect, [and a] willingness to listen."[24] Following Eve Sedgwick's notion of a reparative rather than paranoid orientation and Ricoeur's hermeneutics of listening, this project takes seriously the enterprise of empathetic engagement in an age of cynicism and polarization. As a reaction to such trends, it represents a needed balance of rhetorical theories and writing practices that offer ways of countering apathy and the paralysis of anger and cynicism. Rhetorical empathy balances and sustains. There is a place for both critique and repair, for exposing the workings of power and for resisting the temptation to use the tactics of those we critique. I see rhetorical empathy as both a seeing against and a seeing with—a practice that involves both critical and connected readings.

As appealing as empathy is, it also is rife with complexity: empathy shown by those with power can suggest manipulation, and empathy shown by those with less power can lead to acquiescence and potentially reinforce power imbalances. In postmodern theory, the use of solidarity or empathy by those occupying a dominant subject position has come to be suspect as at least patronizing and at worst manipulative. In *Language and*

Power, Norman Fairclough argues that whenever an individual or group occupying a dominant subject position in a rhetorical situation uses rhetoric characterized by empathy, it is only because that person or group has been forced to by those with less power. In other words, no one would willingly give up power or privilege unless it were in their best interests to do so (to whatever degree we give these up when we become vulnerable to someone with less power). For those with little power within intersectional subject positions, taking a stance of rhetorical empathy risks further vulnerability. This risk is real and should not be ignored; however, such a stance also offers the potential for greater perspective and personal strength.

Following Krista Ratcliffe's work in *Rhetorical Listening*, the book to which this project owes the most debt, I focus on both identifications and differences between interlocutors and acknowledge that struggle and rhetorical negotiations are always already present in discourse. I don't deny that power is always present and that the nature of rhetorical praxis is rooted in the effort to change others or circumstances in some way. All discourse works to shape us in some fashion, and rhetoric-as-change is a vital aspect of rhetorical studies and pedagogy—perhaps the most important function of rhetoric. My point is not to ignore this reality but to push against it and argue for a different way of being-with-others, contributing to Ratcliffe's call for scholars in rhetoric and composition to "map more theoretical terrain and provide more pragmatic tactics for peaceful, cross-cultural negotiation and coalition building."[25] Rhetorical empathy builds on her work, shifting the focus of rhetoric from (only) changing an audience to changing oneself (as well) and extending rhetorical listening in new directions by accounting for the role of the personal and the emotions in rhetorical exchange.

In teaching stories such as Lindquist's, it's important to keep in mind that even though teachers inhabit one subject position that involves power in a classroom—albeit an important one—our power invested by the institution is only one aspect of our identities. Teachers also, of course, may be in less privileged subject positions otherwise in terms of ableness, gender, race, class, or sexual orientation. Power and privilege are slippery concepts that shift in relation to context. A major goal of Ratcliffe's rhetorical listening is acknowledging privilege and getting to a place where someone realizes that how they approach argument is affected by social positioning and deep, historical narratives that play out in every rhetorical situation. People in nondominant subject positions are acutely aware of their social roles and positioning, as Jacqueline Jones Royster points out in "When the First Voice You Hear Is Not Your Own," and must learn early in life to listen to the dominant majority in order to survive. Those with privilege must learn to listen and acknowledge their power.

Like Lynch, I argue in this book that the promise of empathy remains despite its constraints: the multiple, shifting, and intersecting identities constituted in the *I* of discourse can connect with those that constitute the Other to a degree that both experience identification and are changed in some fashion. This can happen not *despite* but *because of* the highlighting of the body and difference, as Lynch argues in "Rhetorics of Proximity: Empathy in Temple Grandin and Cornel West." In the midst of his qualifications of empathy's potential, Lynch suggests that because of its ability to open up new avenues for rhetorical invention, we should at least "make the effort to empathize" and to "approximate empathy."[26] He points out the need for further work in developing theories that "thicken our understanding"[27] of the concept of empathy while incorporating the insights of postmodern theory with "the body squarely at the center of rhetorical exchange."[28]

METHOD AND SITES OF STUDY

My rhetorical analysis of examples in the book, particularly in the gay-rights chapter where I started my research and for which I coded hundreds of pages of online discourse between gay-rights activists and social conservatives, helped me identify the following four characteristics of rhetorical empathy:

- Yielding to an Other by sharing and listening to personal stories
- Considering motives behind speech acts and actions
- Engaging in reflection and self-critique
- Addressing difference, power, and embodiment

I use these four characteristics to analyze the following examples of rhetorical empathy:

- Appeals for justice and better working conditions for domestic workers in Gilded Age Chicago and contemporary Brazil, brought to light in one of Jane Addams's earliest speeches in 1893 and in the social media stories of labor and race activist Joyce Fernandes
- Rhetorical negotiations between gay-rights activist Justin Lee and evangelical Christians
- Composition pedagogies based on principles of rhetorical empathy

Two of the examples focus on rhetorical exchanges in online settings, an environment many consider the most toxic and polarizing space imaginable. We typically associate the internet with echo chambers of people listening and speaking only to those who believe as they do. While this is true in many respects, I find potential for enactments of rhetorical empathy in the multimodality of the web and its user participation, which I demonstrate in the case studies. Furthermore, unlike essays, book-length nonfiction, novels, or speeches, online discursive spaces provide the opportunity to analyze both a text and its reception. Unlike most online discourse, in the sites I analyze, readers may find they want to read the comments; in fact, they may find the comments the most interesting aspect of the exchange. Along with interviews with the writers and activists themselves about their rhetorical choices, the responses of their interlocutors make possible a triangulated analysis of rhetorical exchanges.

Chapter 1, "A Brief History of Empathy," tells the story of empathy's contested significations and its circulation, positioning it within several historical and rhetorical traditions. In the case of a familiar concept such as empathy, it's important to establish which definition(s) of the word *empathy* I rely on and what exactly I mean by the term *rhetorical empathy* in order to clarify how I interpret the texts and rhetorical exchanges in this book. I highlight the semantic distinctions between how the signifiers *empathy*, *sympathy*, and *pity* have circulated historically. In his English translation of *On Rhetoric*, for example, George Kennedy chooses "pity" to translate the closest concept to empathy in Aristotle, the emotion eleos.[29] In the Christian New Testament, however, *eleos* appears twenty-seven times in the original Greek and often is translated as "compassion" or "mercy," including in Luke 10:37 in the parable of the Good Samaritan, wherein Jesus tells Jewish religious leaders that ethnic and political Others are their neighbors, whom they are to care for despite their differences, a fitting signification for the kind of work I associate with rhetorical empathy.[30]

As LuMing Mao points out, our tendency in the West to foreground our arguments and definitions is itself a relic of our Aristotelian rhetorical tradition.[31] A search instead for a contextualization of a concept—where and how a concept has circulated and to what consequences—follows the more indirect, analogy-based epistemologies of Chinese rhetorical traditions. I explore how empathy and related concepts have circulated in canonical rhetorical theories in the West and in others beyond those in the Euro-American rhetorical tradition, including the concept of *bian*, or "argument," in Chinese; the Nyaya Sutra, an ancient Indian text on argument; and the practice of *ṣulḥ* in Arab-Islamic rhetorical traditions. I discuss empathy's roots in late nineteenth-century German aesthetics and its circulation within psychological discourses in the twentieth century. I establish the ways in which rhetorical empathy builds on strands of twentieth-century rhetorical theories, particularly feminist theory. Traditional Euro-American rhetorical theory has most often been about how to gain power over or persuade an audience. The goal of rhetoric within patriarchal systems and established in Aristotle is to defeat an opponent through persuading him (certainly a *him*) that your position, and by extension you, are superior. The change that results from rhetoric lies in your audience, not within yourself. Feminist rhetorical theories and rhetorical praxis beyond the Euro-American tradition, however, challenge these warrants and practices. Rhetorical empathy builds on such valuable work based on listening and understanding, the use of personal narratives, and a willingness to yield in a stance of self-risk and vulnerability, situating rhetoric as an ethical way of negotiating difference rather than an attempt to win a battle or gain power over others.

In chapter 2, "Threads of Feminist Rhetorical Practices: Storytelling and Empathy from Gilded Age Chicago to Facebook," I consider the relationship between digital media and feminist rhetorical practices such as listening and the use of personal stories. I compare the rhetoric of two activists—Jane Addams in Gilded Age Chicago and Joyce Fernandes in contemporary Brazil, who are separated by over a century, social class, and networked technologies with global scope—using the lens of rhetorical empathy. I examine how rhetorical empathy functions within the site of labor-rights rhetoric in one of Jane Addams's earliest speeches, focusing on rhetorical empathy as the ethical and epistemological basis of her rhetoric. Her embodied rhetorical praxis of empathetic rhetoric is as relevant now as it was over a hundred years ago during the Progressive Era, despite her relative obscurity in the United States public today beyond small pockets in the academic world and in Chicago, where she helped establish the social settlement Hull House in 1889 and where the bulk of her life's work occurred. As the Occupy Wall Street protests of 2011 highlighted, income disparity between top earners and the rest of the US population has grown exponentially over the past few decades, drawing comparisons to the Gilded Age (1875–1900). I focus on her first speech on labor rights: "Domestic Service," delivered at the World's Columbian Exhibition in 1893 in Chicago, an early example of her mediating rhetorical style.

I compare Addams's use of rhetorical empathy to the activism of Fernandes, a Brazilian rapper, history teacher, and former domestic worker who has brought attention to the plight of domestic workers in Brazil by featuring their stories on Facebook and Twitter. She's now a pop star in Brazil, appearing on both MTV and a TEDx Talk in Sao Paolo, as well as media outlets around the world after she began posting the stories of domestic laborers on Facebook in July 2016. Her story was picked up by the BBC in early August, and the Facebook page she created to share the stories of other women like herself, "Eu, Empregada Doméstica" ("I, Housemaid"), was a sensation, with over one hundred thousand followers almost overnight.[32] In the BBC article, Fernandes called Eu, Empregada Doméstica a place to "expose what is being swept under the carpet," advocating for improved working conditions and ultimately an end to domestic service as a "vestige of slavery." She approaches her audience of other young women like herself and women who employ domestic workers as one who knows intimately about the suffering and journeys she writes about. This additional element of her subject position and experience adds power to her rhetorical appeal based on personal experience.

Chapter 3, "Rhetorical Empathy in the Gay-Rights/Religious Divide," builds on and complicates Sharon Crowley's exploration of ways progressives can engage with fundamentalists in *Toward a Civil Discourse*. This chapter formed the starting point for the conclusions and theory I offer in the book: it features an exchange centered on one of the most polarizing issues in the United States, and arguably worldwide: support for full inclusion of LGBTQ people in society and support for traditional expressions of gender on the basis of religious belief. I analyze rhetorical exchanges between gay-rights activist and author Justin Lee and his interlocutors on the website of activist, blogger, and popular religious writer Rebecca Held Evans. I also analyze transcripts of interviews I conducted with Lee about his writing and rhetorical strategies.

My research on this topic not only was the exigency for my interest in a way of engaging across difference, but the close examination I did of rhetorical exchanges between gay-rights activists who identify as Christian and those in evangelical communities who resist LGBTQ rights provided the data with which I identified recurring features of rhetorical empathy. Considering the various ways evangelicals in the United States have opposed humane treatment of gay people, including their support of the so-called religious-freedom bills in reaction to the Windsor Supreme Court case legalizing marriage equality in 2013, the question of how to narrow the divide between religious conservatives and queer people and allies remains kairotic.

Chapter 4, "Beyond 'Common Ground': Rhetorical Empathy in Composition Pedagogies," turns from rhetoric in transnational, mostly online settings to the site of college composition, focusing on ways of fostering engagement across difference in the classroom. Current pedagogies in writing studies focusing on argument often neglect the role of the personal within political arguments. Approaches to writing based on the well-known feminist mantra that the personal is political and on what Michael Polanyi calls "personal knowledge" are valuable means of engaging across difference. Such personal epistemologies and writing have been downplayed in composition courses focused on professionalizing students and on argumentation as a primary genre in recent years. In this chapter I trace threads of rhetorical empathy in recent composition theories and share an example of a mixed-genre assignment based on principles of rhetorical empathy in my classes at Baruch College at the City University of New York. The narrative argument assignment on which I focus draws from elements of literacy narratives and argument and builds on students' own experiences and stories, connecting them to larger issues outside the classroom that affect their lives.

First-year composition represents the only site on a national level with the potential to produce, in John Duffy's words, "virtuous arguments."[33] He points out that first-year writing "is not typically associated with improving public discourse, much less considered a 'movement.' For students required to take the course, it may initially be seen as a speed bump, an exercise in curricular gatekeeping best dispatched as painlessly as possible." The reality is that each semester around twenty million students take these required courses, a staple of college curricula he calls "the closest thing we have in American public life to a National Academy of Reasoned Rhetoric, a venue in which students can rehearse the virtues of argument so conspicuously lacking in our current political debates." Composition pedagogies based on rhetorical empathy ask students to recognize the contextual and personally situated nature of all arguments and discourse, allowing a more nuanced, ethical avenue of approaching argument and accounting for the role of emotion and the personal in persuasion and change.

1

A BRIEF HISTORY OF EMPATHY

Confucius's disciple Zigong asks him, "Is there one expression that can be acted upon until the end of one's days?" / "The Master replied, 'There is shu: do not impose on others what you yourself do not want.'"

Confucius, *Analects*

This feeling of becoming is always synonymous with a weakening or renunciation of the self, while in its expansive form . . . it is synonymous with a strengthening and liberation of the self.

Robert Vischer, "On the Optical Sense of Form: A Contribution to Aesthetics," in *Empathy, Form, and Space: Problems in German Aesthetics, 1873–1893*, on the first usage of the word and concept *Einfuhlung* (empathy)

Empathy was not popular with Republicans on the Senate Judiciary Committee when Sonia Sotomayor was a candidate for Supreme Court justice in 2009. In selecting his first nominee to the court, President Obama famously said, "I will seek someone who understands justice isn't about some abstract legal theory or footnote in a case book; it is also about how our laws affect the daily realities of people's lives, whether they can make a living and care for their families, whether they feel safe in their homes and welcome in their own nation. I view that quality of empathy, of understanding and identifying with people's hopes and struggles, as an essential ingredient for arriving at just decisions and outcomes."[1] A Fox News headline during her confirmation hearing read "Obama Pushes for 'Empathetic' Supreme Court Justices"—the scare quotes suggesting that it may be a bit odd for a judge on the highest court in the land

DOI: 10.7330/9781607329107.c001

to have empathy. The piece quotes Wendy Long, a lawyer for a nonprofit group advocating for conservative Supreme Court nominees who served as Charence Thomas's law clerk for a time: "President Obama has referred to this nice word empathy. . . . A judge is supposed to have empathy for no one but simply to follow the law."[2]

In one of the many critiques of empathy during her hearings, Senator John Cornyn declared that Sotomayor must "prove her commitment to impartially deciding cases based on the law, rather than based on her own personal politics, feelings, and preferences."[3] In 2001, Sotomayor discussed the value of personal experience as a judge in a speech at the UC Berkeley law school, stating, "I would hope that a wise Latina woman, with the richness of her experiences, would more often than not reach a better conclusion than a white male who hasn't lived that life."[4] Cornyn's argument, of course, erases the personal; it assumes that total objectivity in interpreting the law is possible, that white, male judges are impartial, and, more perniciously, it ignores the idea that one's body and experiences are not only inescapable but are actually valuable ways we form judgments. The Republican senators' invectives against empathy were a thinly veiled argument that the kind of experience Sotomayor represents does not belong on the court.

Debates about the degree to which our embodied experience affects how we make judgments can be traced back to the origins of Euro-American epistemology in classical Greece. In Book 2 of *On Rhetoric*, Aristotle argues that *ethos* and *pathos* are "non-essentials" for sound judgment. Clear reasoning is not based on rhetorical deliberation grounded in one's experience and emotions but rather in logic, enacted through detached, syllogistic reasoning. Even *logos* or enthymemic reasoning that rhetoric represents—the lower form of reasoning beneath dialectic and logic in his view—is to be used to appeal to the weaknesses of a judge or jury (or anyone a rhetor wishes to persuade). The idea that compassion would play an essential role in judgment and sound reasoning was anathema, as was the idea that anyone from the wrong class—certainly not lower classes or women—would form the kinds of judgments available to elite males.

It's now a commonly held premise, in theory at least among academics and certainly among feminists, that interpretative reasoning is subjective, based on one's social class, on embodied, lived experiences, and on a variety of other factors that must be weighed against the same factors in others. The concept of rhetorical empathy attempts to explain this principle and account for the emotional and personal aspects of judgment. It is, at its core, about the relationship between rhetoric and ethics, a deliberative praxis that offers ways of being-with-others. My own embodied experiences—my life in a female body and especially what I experienced when I came out and identified with a marginalized group—and my research on empathy as a rhetorical concept over the past several years have led me to believe engaging with the Other is one of the primary purposes of rhetoric. In the case of issues that represent fundamental or especially challenging differences—either in belief or intersectional subject positions—this purpose for rhetoric is all the more important.

My purpose in this chapter, and in this project more broadly, is to resist aspects of Aristotelian rhetorical theory that have been tremendously influential in Euro-American culture. In this effort, I explore how empathy and similar concepts have circulated and functioned rhetorically, looking at prominent canonical rhetorical texts in the Euro-American tradition as well as rhetorical texts and traditions beyond it for perspective.[5] In doing so, I follow a method described by Mao of tracing *where* and *how* a concept has circulated and to what consequences, in keeping with more indirect, analogy-based epistemologies characteristic of Chinese rhetorical traditions I discuss below (rather than using primarily analytical and definitional methodologies and topoi of the classical Greco Roman tradition).[6] I pursue a number of paths that intersect in important ways, all of which have bearing on rhetorical empathy. I introduce these paths here and explore them more fully in this chapter.

1. I argue, following David L. Hall and Roger T. Ames in *Anticipating China: Thinking Through the Narratives of Chinese and Western Culture*, that classical Greek rhetoric, with its focus on agonistic aims for rhetoric, continues to structure the practice of rhetoric and being-with-others (the current political divide as an example).

2. More focus is needed to expand the rhetorical canon beyond Euro-American rhetorics in keeping with efforts to decolonize education described by Marie Battiste. Rhetorical empathy builds on elements of global rhetorics beyond the agonistic Greek tradition, representing an alternative to rhetoric-as-persuasion and a feminist challenge to the denigration of the personal and emotion as valuable epistemologies. Classical Chinese and Arab-Islamic traditions, for example, offer alternative ways of thinking about the role of rhetoric as persuasion, situating rhetoric instead as peacemaking and as relational engagements across difference, furthering the project of destabilizing "power-over," agonistic rhetoric in favor of "being-with."

3. Classical Greek epistemology, centered on Plato and Aristotle and hierarchal in nature, has promoted the idea of one right answer. Within this way of thinking, the purpose of rhetoric has been either to find an objective truth or convince an Other that one's view of the truth (or even the best truth) is one they should accept.

4. The discussion of eleos in Book 2 of Aristotle's *On Rhetoric* (translated as "pity" in the most widely circulating versions) as socially situated rather than a universal psychological affect has echoes of current theories of the political nature of emotion. This earliest treatment of the social function of emotions has a great deal of bearing on how we currently think of emotions, although I push against viewing Aristotle simply as explanatory or descriptive rather than as normative (which I explain below).

5. One of the most famous passages in the Christian faith on the ethics of being-with-others features the same Greek word, *eleos*, that appears in Book 2 of Aristotle's *On Rhetoric*. The parable of the Good Samaritan positions the Other as having the same worth as those closest to us and challenges the idea that we (should) only extend compassion to those for whom we feel sorry or out of threat to ourselves (as in Aristotle) or to those we most care about (as in Hume).

6. To further distinguish empathy from pity, I highlight the semantic distinctions between how the signifiers *empathy*, *sympathy*, and *pity* have circulated historically.[7]

7. Related to Aristotle's treatment of pity, David Hume in *A Treatise on Human Nature* formulated what has come to be known as the *theory of concentric circles*, the idea that we care most about those closest to us and are most persuaded by their suffering or potential suffering, arguing that empathy (what he calls "sympathy") is the basis for ethics.

8. The concept of empathy as we know it originated in nineteenth-century German aesthetics as an attempt to explain how we are changed by an emotional identification with nature through art.

9. Modern and postmodern rhetorical theories, beginning in the early twentieth century up to the present, represent both a recovery of Aristotle (Corbett, Kinneavy) and a challenge to Aristotle's rhetoric-as-persuasion (Richards, Burke, Booth, and others).

10. Rhetorical empathy draws on feminist rhetorical theories that connect the personal and the political and that keep the body and intersectional power relations at the center of all critique.

CHALLENGING CLASSICAL WESTERN VALUES

Rhetorical empathy represents a stark contrast to what George Kennedy describes as the "contentiousness" of the dominant Euro-American classical rhetorical tradition: "The Greeks were contentious from the beginning, and acceptance and indulgence of open contention and rivalry has remained a characteristic of Western society, except when suppressed by powerful authority of church or state."[8] Kennedy characterizes the canonical Euro-American rhetorical tradition, handed down by the Athenians, as eristic, focused on rivalries and winning. "Life was regarded as a contest"[9] in which debates and athletic events became popular forms of public expression and entertainment. He compares this tradition to the rhetorical traditions of the Middle East, India, and China, in which, he argues, consensus and avoiding conflict have traditionally been valued.[10]

In *Anticipating China,* David L. Hall and Roger T. Ames argue that the shape of the Euro-American intellectual culture has been "importantly determined" by ideas invented or discovered in the period beginning with the Greeks in 500–300 BCE and culminating with Augustine in the fifth century CE. They create a heuristic that holds a great deal of explanatory power for understanding the intellectual foundations of Euro-American and Chinese epistemologies:

- **First-problematic thinking (China):** characterized by analogical or correlative thinking, listening, harmony, open-endedness, subjectivity, vagueness, metaphor, experience, relationships, metonymy; focused on change rather than fixity and on contexts, localized meanings, particulars rather than generalities or universals; has no determinant or causal structure

- **Second-problematic thinking (Euro-American):** characterized by causal thinking, first principles based on unified source of being (God/personified agency or source), abstractions, definitions, logic, rationality, Enlightenment-influenced philosophies based on quests for origins, patterns, regularity; focused on being, resting, hierarchies, taxonomies; being valued over becoming

While they point out that China and the West have elements of both first- and second-problematic thinking, they argue that first-problematic thinking is "importantly present" in Chinese culture and second-problematic thinking is dominant in the Western philosophical tradition, "present in such a way that it significantly qualifies, defines, or otherwise shapes the culture."[11]

What Hall and Ames call second-problematic thinking has, of course, come under much scrutiny over the past century, especially over the past few decades by postmodern and poststructuralist theorists such as Michel Foucault and Jacques Derrida. Hall and Ames discuss the fact that postmodern philosophy is similar in many respects to prominent strains of Chinese thought. For example, such theories have critiqued Enlightenment rationality, the quest for origins and first principles, the supremacy of logic, and the linear progress of (Western) civilization—all characteristics of Hall and Ames's second-problematic thinking.

Second-problematic thinking is patriarchal in its stress on taxonomies that function as hierarchies, its valuation of logic over emotion, its association with essentialism over becoming, and in its devaluing of socially contingent epistemologies. In her work on recovering the Sophists, Susan Jarratt writes that "the character projected onto the feminine as 'other' shares with Plato's sophists qualities of irrationality (or non-rationality), magical or hypnotic power, subjectivity, emotional sensitivity; all these are devalued in favor of their 'masculine' or philosophic opposites—rationality, objectivity, detachment and so on."[12]

As Hall and Ames point out, studying rhetorical traditions outside the dominant Euro-American canon can not only help students and scholars of rhetoric enlarge our knowledge of the value of such traditions in their own right but also can help us see our own practices with new eyes, making the familiar unfamiliar and helping disrupt the dominance of what is importantly present. Keith Lloyd's study of the epistemology and rhetorical reasoning in the Nyaya Sutra, for example, an ancient Indian text on argument (200 BCE–450 AD), suggests the goal of rhetoric in the Nyaya is discussion, inquiry and consensus, contributing toward the goals in Hindu philosophy of harmony and self-abnegation, with the rhetor's goal not self-expression, persuasion, or winning but a "seeing together."[13] These goals are markedly different than the second-problematic thinking of Euro-American traditions and strikingly similar to important rhetorical practices in Chinese and Arab-Islamic traditions.

CHINESE RHETORICAL TRADITIONS

Although no single character in Chinese "corresponds" directly with a Western notion of rhetoric as we understand it in classical Greek terms, one important character representing the idea of rhetoric in ancient China (of several outlined by Xing Lu and Hall and Ames) is *bian*, translated loosely in English as "argument." The practice of *bian* itself is associated with interdependence rather than contention and polarity. Lu in *Rhetoric in Ancient China: Fifth to Third Century BCE*, describes *bian* as "a spontaneous activity capable of bridging opposites and achieving the dao. The activity of bian, accordingly, was not polarizing; nor did it consist of imposing one's view on others. Instead, bian was a process for connecting and transcending apparent differences and polarized positions."[14] Among the multiple definitions and representations of the Western term *rhetoric* that appear in classical Chinese texts, *bian* is one of the most prominent. Chinese rhetoric should not and cannot be reduced to simply nonagonistic exchange, but the fact that a concept such as *bian* plays such a prominent role in the Chinese rhetorical tradition is significant.

The Confucian disciple Xunzi is, according to Hall and Ames, the most closely aligned of Chinese thinkers with the Sophists in the Western tradition, and elements of his thinking and approach to rhetoric closely align with principles of feminist theory and rhetorical empathy. Hall and Ames argue that for Xunzi,

> ideally, dispute is a cooperative exercise among responsible participants that leads to a search for alternatives upon which all can agree. There is a fundamental disesteem for coercion of any kind, since aggressiveness or violence threatens to disrupt rather than reinforce or improve upon the existing social order. After all, the goal of protest is not victory in contest, which is necessarily divisive, but the strengthening of communal harmony.[15]

Peter T. Coleman, director of the International Center for Cooperation and Conflict Resolution at Columbia, points to the role of culturally influenced ways of thinking and behaving in exchanges across seemingly intractable political and social difference. With echoes of Hall and Ames's first- and second-problematic thinking, Coleman points to the work of psychologists Kaiping Peng and Richard E. Nisbett in "Culture, Dialectics, and Reasoning about Contradiction." They hold that "Chinese ways of dealing with seeming contradictions result in a dialectical or compromise approach—retaining basic elements of opposing perspectives by seeking a 'middle way.' On the other hand, European-American ways, deriving from a lay version of Aristotelian logic, result in a differentiation model that polarizes contradictory perspectives in an effort to determine which fact or position is correct."[16] Like the yin-yang symbol, the focus in Confucian-influenced philosophical systems is toward finding ways of working together; elements of different ways of thinking are integrated rather than one being displaced. Most important, the contradictions and differences are part of one another. There is no entirely good or entirely bad, no entirely right or entirely wrong position; there are multiple positions, and they can learn from one another. This way of thinking goes refreshingly against the pro-versus-con way of thinking many of our students bring with them to our classes and into which we're enculturated at an early age in the shadow of Aristotelian logic.

Furthermore, in Chinese epistemology, emotions not only are not looked down upon in deliberation, they are highly valued. Robert Solomon writes that how a culture talks about emotions forms what he calls the "emotional portrait" of that culture. He points out that in Chinese epistemology, emotions often are associated with *chi* (power or energy), one of the most important concepts in Chinese philosophy. Echoing recent work in cultural studies and rhetorical theory on affect by Sara Ahmed, Daniel Gross, and Susan Miller, Solomon argues that emotions are judgments, always based on a certain perspective and always defined in part from one's physical embodiment, one's place in the world, and one's cultural context and roles. Judgments/emotions are culturally taught, cognitively framed, and intrinsic to experience.[17]

In "Confucian Silence and Remonstration," Arabella Lyon points to ways in which Chinese epistemology stresses community over the individual, noting that in Chinese rhetoric, the Descartian mind/body and emotion/reason split emphasizing the individual self, "I think therefore I am," becomes the communal "We relate, therefore we are."[18] The role of the Other in forming one's own identity has echoes of Diane Davis's arguments in *Inessential Solidarity* about the primacy of rhetoric in forming the self. There is no *I*, in other words, without a *Thou*: "It's not so much that the subject responds to alterity . . . but that 'the subject' *is* the response to alterity. It has no substance beyond this inessential solidarity, this receptivity and responsivity that are the conditions for symbolic exchange."[19] Rhetoric, she writes, is first philosophy: "The generative power of the trope is the ground for all thought."[20] Following Emmanuel Levinas, the "something" prior to communication is not the isolated self of Kenneth Burke (the division after the fall in metaphorical terms) but rather a body interacting with another, an exposed-ness, a vulnerability, and an underlying "obligation to respond" that forms the basis of all ethics—the face of the Other. The implications for ethical action and responsiveness to the Other in this way of thinking are profound. The Other literally is part of me and vice versa, rhetorically and epistemologically speaking.

ARAB-ISLAMIC TRADITIONS

Rasha Diab in *Shades of Ṣulḥ* explores an important rhe-torical practice focused on peacemaking and reconciliation within Arab-Islamic traditions. An ancient mediation practice grounded in Islamic principles of conflict negotiation, the practice of *ṣulḥ* involves a wronged person and their oppressor working with a mediator to ensure justice for the victim, recon-ciliation for the wrongdoer, and a sense of peace among mem-bers of a community. The practice, designed to avoid cycles of revenge, still is used in nonurban areas functioning outside formal court systems. Diab explains that highlighting aspects of Islamic traditions centered on peacemaking "intersect[s] with" critiques of "power (ab)use, (coercive) silencing, exclusion-ary practices, the politics of persuasion, and power relations embedded in genres" and "seeks to underline facilitative condi-tions as well as reflective, communicative practices that seek and promote identification, cooperation, and duties to dialogue, listen, assume prudence, and reflect on and embrace silence."[21] Storytelling and bearing witness are important elements in ṣulḥ to ensure victims are heard. An underlying premise for the practice of ṣulḥ entails the oppressor listening to the victim and offering to make amends, ideally offering an apology and acknowledging wrongdoing.

At the same time, the wrongdoer is treated ethically as well, with the primary goal restorative rather than punitive justice.[22]

Diab explains that in some cases, such as the Sierra Leone civil war from 1991 to 2002, former child soldiers who had been "abducted, conscripted, and often compelled to commit acts of killing, mutilation, rape, and abduction"[23] were reintegrated into the community through a practice of ṣulḥ, with the ethnographic researcher noting that in the process "they chose to remember that the child ex-combatant was a victim, too."[24] As Diab explains, "Traditional peacemaking practices, like ṣulḥ, are grounded in a worldview that elevates relational responsibility and understands justice and peace after violation as exceeding the punishment of a wrongdoer (i.e., punitive justice)."[25]

A number of characteristics of ṣulḥ bear highlighting for their resonance with rhetorical empathy. First, the dual goals of ṣulḥ rhetoric are justice and peace: justice for those who are wronged and peace for the wrongdoer and the community. These goals resonate a great deal with rhetorical empathy's dual goals of seeing with and seeing against—both a critical and a restorative/connected reading of the Other. Diab points to these dual goals as characteristic of restorative models and to the importance of both: "I refer to the former [justice] as critique *against* and the latter [peace] as critique *for*. Both modes of critique are interdependent; investing in the critique against violence/injustice is not enough, for we equally need to invest in the critique for peace, an investment that articulates and makes actionable a vision for peace and justice."[26]

Second, Diab compares the rhetoric of ṣulḥ to Edward Corbett's "rhetoric of the open hand"; in Arabic, the terms used for shaking hands, reconciliation, and eating together are similar and name "crucial social acts with conspicuous relational goals that counter the logic of violence/violation/alienation and begin the work of peaceful coexistence."[27] Third, Diab draws on Ratcliffe's notion of rhetorical listening to explain how victims share their stories and are responded to by those who have wronged them. A final element of ṣulḥ practices that holds importance for comparative purposes is self-critique, or self-care, depending on the circumstances: "Internal reconciliation between warring factions of the self is a precursor to, condition of, and model for the resolution of world conflicts and the establishment of a cooperative international community of peace pursuers."[28] Her analysis of the dialogue *The Great Court of Ṣulḥ*, written by Muhammad Madi Abu al-Aaim (1869–1937), a theologian and professor of Islamic law, suggests that the following three characteristics comprise what she calls "a culturally inflected, rhetorical method for reconciliation": (1) bidirectional discourse: those who are grieved share their stories and those who have been associated with harm listen to those stories; (2) "introspective, reflective discourse"; and (3) a visionary discourse for the future.[29]

In any comparative-rhetoric endeavor it's important to keep in mind the notion of etic/emic (global/local) approaches, which Mao describes as a way of deeply contextualizing rhetorical practices by "moving between self and other, the local and the global, and the contingencies of the present and the historical imperatives of the past."[30] In other words, on an emic (local) level, it's important to acknowledge aspects of ṣulḥ that are culturally specific within Arab-Islamic communities. On an etic (global) level, it's important to avoid simply comparing such rhetorics to the Euro-American tradition but rather to take them on their own terms and ideally learn from them in order to imagine new ways of thinking beyond second-problematic values in classical Greco-Roman rhetoric.

PATHOS AND PERSUASION IN EURO-AMERICAN RHETORICAL TRADITIONS

I turn now to Greco-Roman, Euro-American rhetorical traditions to trace two threads: (1) the history of how the concept of empathy and similar sentiments we associate with empathy today have circulated in this tradition in order to discover what has been, in Hall and Ames's model, "importantly present" in this tradition and (2) the relationship between pathos and persuasion/change; that is, the relationship between empathy and rhetoric.

Aristotle

Martin Heidegger calls Aristotle's treatment of *pathos* or emotions in Book 2 of *On Rhetoric* as "the first systematic hermeneutic of the everydayness of Being with one another."[31] The emotion eleos in Book 2, chapter 8, which all prominent translators of Aristotle have associated with pity, was a virtue personified by the Greek goddess Eleos, often depicted as grief-stricken and in tears. Her counterpart for the Romans was the goddess Clemency, a concept associated by the *Oxford English Dictionary* with "mercy, leniency, lenience, mildness, indulgence, forbearance, quarter, compassion, humanity, pity, sympathy, kindness, magnanimity, benignity, charity, grace, humaneness, humanitarianism, soft-heartedness, and tenderness."

This emotion, the closest concept to empathy in Aristotle, could be thought of as the very basis of the humanities—the ability not only to imagine what others have experienced but to be moved by it to an extent that we're both enlarged and humbled at the same time. As Susan Keen notes in *Empathy and the Novel*, "Empathy seems so basic a human trait that lacking it can be seen as a sign of inhumanity;" Keen points to Ridley Scott's 1992 film *Blade Runner*, based on Philip K. Dick's *Do Androids Dream of Electric Sheep?*, which explores the idea of empathy as "the one essential, recognizable trait of humanity."[32]

Aristotle's treatment of emotion in *On Rhetoric* is thoroughly social and rhetorical—that is, political—relevant for current theories of the political function of emotion (Ahmed, Gross). Aristotle describes pity not as a psychological attribute but rather as an emotion that circulates socially and influences people based on their position in relation to others. Emotions for Aristotle are performative and audience dependent, not "natural" states of mind. As with his treatment of other emotions of anger, fear, shame, kindness, and envy, his discussion of pity centers on who is likely to feel pity, for whom one is likely to experience it, and in what circumstances.

Those who likely are to feel pity include:

- those who have also suffered and escaped
- older people because of their practical wisdom and experience
- the weak and the cowardly
- the educated "for they are discerning"
- those with family members who also could suffer and therefore cause suffering to the subject

Those who do not feel pity include:

- men (women and slaves were not considered human) who are "utterly ruined feel no pity—they think there is nothing left for them to suffer"
- those who are "enormously happy" because they think it beyond them to suffer evil and they lack a sense of vulnerability
- those experiencing certain emotional states such as anger or confidence (because they do not consider the future); violent insolence (they do not care if something happens to them or others); and fear (they are taken up by their own suffering)
- those who do not believe good people exist in the world and who therefore believe everyone is worthy of suffering[33]

Those for whom pity is felt include:

- friends
- people like themselves (in age, in character, in habits, in rank, in birth because people pity others who experience things they think might also happen to them)
- people who suffer from events or circumstances that seem realistic or imminent to the subject
- people who do not deserve to suffer[34]

In his descriptions of the motives or causes for someone experiencing eleos, he focuses on the fear of a similar suffering or fate happening to the self, connecting the appeal to eleos primarily with self-preservation rather than to ethical actions.[35] His descriptions of the social situatedness of emotions are grounded in cultural values associated with certain kinds of people. For example, those we decide do not deserve to suffer are deemed worthy of pity, which is determined for us by the values of those in the discourse community upon whose judgments we depend for the creation and affirmation of our identities.

The degree to which emotions are socially and culturally encoded becomes clear through contemporary examples such as gay rights. Much of the rhetoric surrounding gay rights from conservatives, especially religious conservatives, hinges on their belief that LGBTQ people choose their sexual orientation (in defiance of God-given rules) and therefore suffer numerous psychological, social, even physical (in the case of AIDS) consequences as a result. Decisions about who deserves and does not deserve to suffer become highly politicized debates grounded in emotional attachments to social discourses.

Parable of the Good Samaritan

In my exploration of rhetorical empathy, I focus on the relationship between the subject and the object, particularly how the subject positions or places themself in relation to the object. I situate rhetorical empathy as coming alongside or feeling *into* the experiences of an Other rather than feeling *for* or displacing an Other, usually associated with pity or sympathy. The use of *pity* in Aristotle's discussion of the emotion eleos implies a removed stance that isn't as concerned with the Other in an ethical sense—certainly not in the sense of promoting prosocial, ethical actions—as it is with moving an audience to make judgments almost out of a sense of guilt or fear that "there but for the grace of God go I." While Aristotle's treatment of eleos still holds explanatory power about why we feel pity, it does not hold a great deal of potential for ethical deliberation and action.

Pity's signification as feeling *for* or being somewhat safely removed from an Other often means we remain unchanged; we colonize, we subsume. When we feel *into* another, as empathy often signifies, we identify with an Other to the point that the emotions we experience change us—we begin to experience the Other's world, and it changes our own. This kind of empathy becomes a mutual exchange regardless of how the Other responds.

Eleos appears twenty-seven times in the original Greek New Testament and often is translated as "compassion" or "mercy," including in Luke 10:37 in the parable of the Good Samaritan, one of the most influential texts on ethics in the Christian faith. The rhetorical context of the parable is significant; a lawyer asks Jesus what he must do to inherit eternal life, and Jesus responds with what is known as the Great Commandment: "Thou shalt love the Lord thy God with all thy heart, and with all thy soul, and with all thy strength, and with all thy mind; and thy neighbour as thyself."[36] The Great Commandment appears within the context of the parable of the Good Samaritan, a story in the midst of a Socratic-like exchange in which a lawyer tries to extricate himself from the implications of the radical command, asking, "And who is my neighbour?" The rhetoric in this passage is common in the Gospels: Jesus turns to story rather than syllogistic dialogue, a strategy that functions to disarm the arguments of his interlocutors and make his ethical commands personal.

> [30] And Jesus answering said, A certain man went down from Jerusalem to Jericho, and fell among thieves, which stripped him of his raiment, and wounded him, and departed, leaving him half dead. [31] And by chance there came down a certain priest that way: and when he saw him, he passed by on the other side. [32] And likewise a Levite, when he was at the place, came and looked on him, and passed by on the other side. [33] But a certain Samaritan, as he journeyed, came where he was: and when he saw him, he had compassion on him, [34] And went to him, and bound up his wounds, pouring in oil and wine, and set him on his own beast, and brought him to an inn, and took care of him. [35] And on the morrow when he departed, he took out two pence, and gave them to the host, and said unto him, Take care of him; and whatsoever thou spendest more, when I come again, I will repay thee. [36] Which now of these three, thinkest thou, was neighbour unto him that fell among the thieves? [37] And he said, He that shewed mercy on him. Then said Jesus unto him, Go, and do thou likewise.[37]

The Golden Rule of using care for oneself as a guide to ethical treatment of others is a common thread running through all major ethical and religious traditions. Its close analogue in Chinese rhetoric and ethics is the notion of *shu*. In the *Analects,*

Confucius's disciple Zigong asks him, "Is there one expression that can be acted upon until the end of one's days?"/ "The Master replied, 'There is *shu*: do not impose on others what you yourself do not want.'"[38] The influence of Confucius (551–479 BCE) on Chinese thought and culture at every level, even up to the present day, cannot be overstated. *Shu* in Confucian thought is a method of determining right conduct in relation to others, as described by Hall and Ames, citing Lau: "In morals, it is by means of the method of *shu* that we can hope to be able to practice benevolence, and *shu* consists in using ourselves as analogy to find out about the likes and dislikes of other human beings."[39] *Shu* is central to Confucian right conduct and moral thinking.

Sympathy and Ethics in Campbell and Hume

Corbett argues that rhetoric in the centuries between ancient Greece and Rome and the Enlightenment era was largely focused on logical appeals.

> Although the Renaissance humanists adopted the full panoply of persuasive strategies—the logical, the emotional, and the ethical—they certainly placed the greatest emphasis on the cognitive approach to invention. In none of the Renaissance rhetorics do we find as much attention paid to emotional appeals as Aristotle paid in Book Two of his *Rhetoric*. It is not until the third quarter of the eighteenth century, with the appearance of George Campbell's *The Philosophy of Rhetoric*, which coincided with the growth of interest in faculty psychology, that we find increasing attention being paid to the strategies of the emotional appeal.[40]

For George Campbell in *The Philosophy of Rhetoric*, rhetoric—and the emotions—were not contingent on social situatedness or on inventing ideas to best persuade an audience based on commonplaces but on four purposes: enlightening the understanding, pleasing the imagination, moving the passions, and influencing the will.[41] The boundaries between persuasion and moving an audience's emotions and stirring the imagination with discourse become blurred, however, in his discussion of vivacity—the ability to stir an audience with words that make ideas and experience become real to them, as if they are experiencing them in their imagination. He writes that "the connexion . . . that generally subsisteth between vivacity and belief will appear less marvelous, if we reflect that there is not so great a difference between argument and illustration as is usually imagined. The same ingenious writer says, concerning moral reasoning, that it is but a kind of comparison."[42]

Emotion, personal experience, and rhetorical persuasion converge in vivacity: the greater the ability of a writer or speaker to cause an audience to identify with an experience he (certainly a he) describes, the greater chance of moving them to ends he wishes, a type of "reasoning by experience." Campbell writes that "the ideas of the poet give greater pleasure, command closer attention, operate more strongly on the passions, and are longer remembered" than "a cold but lively historiographer."[43]

Although Hume's work focuses on the operations of the mind as "natural," universal functions, a great deal of resonance exists between Aristotle's conception of emotion as socially situated and Hume's theory that our experience of emotion, specifically sympathy, results from our social position and relationships. In a canonical work on sympathy, *A Treatise on Human Nature*, Hume argues that sympathy[44] is the basis for morality. Hume has become well known for his theory of concentric circles[45] and levels of relationships that influence our emotions and actions. It holds in essence that we have greater emotional attachments to those in our close circle and thus a greater potential to experience a feeling of loss or shame if we disappoint them, for example, than we do with people for whom we have no affection.

Like Campbell, Hume adopts Francis Bacon's appropriation of faculty psychology,[46] which posits that in order to change someone's mind, a rhetor must appeal to various parts of the mind (in Campbell's case the understanding, the imagination, the passions, and the will). Hume argues that the passions (or the emotions), not reason, motivate us to action.[47] In fact, Hume goes so far as to argue that sympathy/empathy is the link between emotion and understanding/thought (what he calls "ideas" and we may now call *ideology*). They differ only in terms of their power or vivacity in the mind, and this vivacity, he argues, comes from the social proximity of two people, the relationship between them.

> In sympathy there is an evident conversion of an idea into an impression. This conversion arises from the relations of objects to ourself. Ourself is always intimately present to us. Let us compare all these circumstances, and we shall find, that sympathy is exactly correspondent to the operations of our understanding; and even contains something more surprizing and extraordinary.[48]

The "surprizing and extraordinary" function of sympathy/empathy, he goes on to argue, is its ability to transform ideas into something more real and epistemologically relevant (i.e., persuasive) to us. Empathy is powerful and transformative because of its proximity to our bodies (i.e., we experience empathy bodily in the form of sensory impressions and also as a secondary impression in the form of an emotion) and to the degree to which we can relate to the one with whom we empathize.

Unlike Aristotle's pity and Hume's treatment of sympathy, those to whom we should show compassion in the parable of the Good Samaritan are not only those closest to us in the common sense of neighbor but are in fact the racial, ethnic, and political Others, as the Samaritans were to the Jews.[49] The rhetoric of the parable is a radical ethic that connects the feeling or experience of love—for God, oneself, and others—to ethical actions. It extends Hume's concentric circles of moral reasoning and ethical actions outward toward those outside the groups with whom we identify racially, ethnically, class-wise, religiously, and otherwise—extending compassion's reach even to our enemies. And it suggests that a diminishing of the self is how such ethical action happens, resulting in an increased ability to identify with those we've Othered, an experience closely related to empathy's origin in the sublime within the context of aesthetics in the late nineteenth century in Germany.

Empathy and Aesthetics

Empathy as a distinct concept arose within the context of late nineteenth-century German aesthetics in an effort by philosopher Robert Vischer to explain how we're changed by an emotional identification with art. In his work *On the Optical Sense of Form: A Contribution to Aesthetics*, Vischer coined *Einfühlung* to signify the idea of feeling one's way into, or feeling with, a work of art. Though the German words are similar, Visher chose not to use the term for identification (*Eisnfühlung*), or *Nachgefühl*, vicarious feelings. For him the experience of being moved and changed by art surpassed the significations of mutual feeling and emotion associated at that time with the word *sympathy* (*Mitgefühl*).[50] In their introduction to Vischer's work, Harry Francis Mallgrave and Eleftherios Ikonomou suggest he developed the term in an attempt to account for "the role that subjective feeling plays in conditioning the perception of form."[51] Vischer led a countermovement against formalism in the study of art and argued for the role of emotion and experience in artistic interpretation, pointing back to Romanticism and theories of the sublime. In doing so, he was attempting to find a middle road between formalism and content, bringing the focus on the viewer/reader/audience rather than the object itself, "considering the subjective content that we—the viewer—bring to aesthetic contemplation."[52]

Although *empathy* in its circulation since his first use of the term has come to be associated with sentimentalism on the one hand and the highest form of ethics on the other (via its connections with compassion and altruism), in its original context in Vischer's work, it was more closely associated with the latter. He saw *Einfühlung* as "a pervasive attitude, an openness that we maintain with the world" and, in its highest sense, as our desire to be connected or in union with all things.[53] In this process, rather than a narcissistic projection of the self onto the Other or a text or image, the self is diminished in a transcendent experience. He associates empathy with motion and change, both a contracting and expanding of the self.

This feeling of becoming is always synonymous with a weakening or renunciation of the self, while in its expansive form . . . it is synonymous with a strengthening and liberation of the self.[54]

The instinct for happiness discovers that the only magical secret of satisfaction is care for the general human welfare. Thus we rise from the simple love of self to a love of family and species (race) and from there to absolute altruism, philanthropy, and the noble sentiments of civic awareness. It is the intimation of the good that enriches love. For this reason concepts such as value, power, and meaning no longer suffice to characterize the mental stimulus concerned. . . . I feel myself in my own and in another's body but only as a worthy representative of the whole species. This advance is actually nothing other than an intellectual renunciation and volatilization of the feeling of self, which now exists only in relation to the whole.[55]

Vischer's original idea of empathy, grounded in aesthetics and spiritual union with art and others—with the universe as a spiritual idea—began to circulate via the English "empathy" as the idea of actively, imaginatively attempting to understand the mind (the experiences and the emotions) of another in the early decades of modern psychology in the U.S. and England. *Empathy* first appeared in English in the early twentieth century in the work of Edward Titchener (1867–1927), a British experimental psychologist who served as professor at Cornell and authored widely circulated psychology textbooks. Fluent in Greek and Latin, Titchener based *empathy* on a translation from the German *Einfühlung* via the Greek *empatheia*.[56] Wispé speculates that Titchener's focus on metaphor and imaginative thinking led him to adopt the German term over the more commonly known *sympathy*, which signified a more passive or removed experience of emotional identification. In *Empathy and the Novel*, Keen associates empathy's origins and the invention of motion pictures, pointing to the relationship between the expansion of semiotic modes and increased empathetic experience, also in the context of art.[57]

During this same period, Sigmund Freud also took up the study of empathy, though his focus primarily lay with identification and failed identifications of the subject with the object. Freud wrote that empathy provided a way of understanding "what is inherently foreign to our ego."[58] In *Civilization and Its Discontents* he describes the experience of being in love, in which the boundary between ego and object threatens to melt away, as a pathology.[59] He admits that he had never experienced the sort of connectedness to all living things that people described to him as "a sensation of 'eternity,' a feeling as of something limitless, unbounded—as it were, 'oceanic'"—although he did not rule it out as a source of motivation based on feelings, which, he admits, "are not easy to deal with scientifically." Freud describes this sense of connectedness as "a purely subjective fact, not an article of faith; it brings with it no assurance of personal immortality, but it is the source of the religious energy which is seized upon by the various Churches and religious systems, directed by them into particular channels, and doubtless also exhausted by them."[60]

Empathetic Threads in Modern and Contemporary Rhetorical Theories

It could be argued that the rise of rhetoric and composition as a disciplinary field in the late twentieth century was based on two competing interests: the first was identifying the field with classical rhetoric, specifically Aristotelian thought, which positions rhetoric as argument (discreet from narrative and literature); the second was the rise of major rhetorical theories that resisted the agonistic, hierarchical origins of Western rhetoric. The focus on Aristotle in the recovery of rhetoric in the mid- to late twentieth century, primarily by Edward Corbett and James Kinneavy, had the effect of linking the teaching of writing to the very origins of Western thought in Aristotle, rhetoric alongside (not beneath) poetics as the foundational theory undergirding a perpetually beleaguered academic discipline.

Central to my aims in exploring rhetorical empathy are the premises that its characteristics are not importantly present in the most dominant rhetorical theory of classical Greece and that second-problematic thinking continues to have tremendous influence in rhetoric and composition and in how we perceive of and engage with the Other. There simply is no escaping

Aristotle, for better or worse. While my own academic training situates rhetoric as the foundation for composition, and while I continue to draw on Aristotelian theory in my own thinking and teaching, I can't deny that the hegemony of Aristotle, both in rhetoric as a field and in our larger culture, has helped maintain the perception and practice of rhetoric as persuasion and argument, a way to change and, at its worst, manipulate and control others.

Prominent strains of rhetorical theory in the twentieth century have shifted the emphasis of rhetoric from persuasion toward understanding (Richards), identification (Burke), finding common ground (Young, Becker, and Pike), and listening (Booth). The most important rhetorical theory after Aristotle in the Euro-American tradition, Burke's identification, has clear implications for destabilizing the idea of power over others as a central goal of rhetoric. Burke repeats Aristotle's definition of rhetoric as the art of persuasion, but he starts prior to persuasion with identification, as he argues all persuasion must begin with some form of identification of the subject with the object of language, of the rhetor with the audience. For Burke, rhetoric is necessary because of divisions and is used to bring about connection and cooperation.

Building on Burke's ideas, Rogerian rhetoric represents the most significant challenge to Aristotelian rhetoric thus far. It was introduced to the burgeoning field of rhetoric and composition in the early 1970s by Richard Young, Alton Becker, and Kenneth Pike and championed by Maxine Hairston at the College Composition and Communication annual meeting in 1976 in Philadelphia. It gained traction in the 1970s and still appears in textbooks as an alternative to an Aristotelian-Toulmin approach to argument. Young, Becker, and Pike developed Rogerian rhetoric in the 1960s as a response to what they felt was a weakness in classical rhetoric: an emphasis on persuasion and defeating an opponent rather than an attempt at learning, connecting, and understanding. In Rogerian rhetoric, the goal of rhetoric is to reduce an audience's sense of threat so they will be open to what the writer has to say and willing to consider alternatives to their own beliefs. In their book *Rhetoric: Discovery and Change*, in which they made a case for this new kind of rhetoric, Young, Becker, and Pike brought the principles of psychotherapist Carl Rogers into composition studies. The core of Rogerian strategy is connecting with an audience, letting them know you understand their beliefs and values. In "Dealing with Breakdowns in Communication," Rogers defines "understanding" as

> seeing the expressed idea and attitude from the other person's point of view, to sense how it feels to him, to achieve his frame of reference in regard to the thing he is talking about. It requires empathy, requires getting inside the other person's skin and see-ing the world through his eyes, or, to speak less metaphorically, it requires considering the beliefs and perspectives of the reader in context of his attitudes, values, and past experiences.[61]

His notion of understanding resonates with Ratcliffe's use of the word in *Rhetorical Listening* to signify the practice of "stand-ing under" the discourse of others in a position of humility. Rogers's underlying theory was that we hold our beliefs because of a sense of threat to our identity and that the first requirement for changing beliefs is to eliminate this sense of threat. Young, Becker, and Pike relied heavily on Burke's theory of identifica-tion (their epigraph for chapter 1 is from Burke's *Rhetoric of Mo-tives*: "Rhetoric is concerned with the state of Babel after the Fall") as well as his theory of rhetoric as "the use of language as a symbolic means of inducing cooperation in beings that by na-ture respond to symbols."[62] Cooperation, not persuasion, was for them the primary focus of rhetoric, and listening and empathy are cornerstones of their rhetorical theory.

Rogerian rhetoric never has had the kind of traction and cir-culation of Aristotelian rhetoric. It has been rightly critiqued from a number of angles, including that it asks women and those in marginalized subject positions to set their own bodies and experiences aside to objectively summarize the arguments of others (Lassner) and that it lacks a sufficiently robust episte-mological basis (Lunsford). The theory and practice I advocate in this book differs from Rogerian rhetoric in that rhetorical

empathy does not remove the personal and the body from rhetorical engagement; rather, it emphasizes them. Further, rhetorical empathy, unlike Rogerian rhetoric, is not formulaic: it
does not prescribe a series of steps or even, at worst, an outline
to follow when writing a position paper.[63]

Like Rogerian rhetoric, Wayne Booth's listening rhetoric
also makes use of empathetic principles. Influenced by I. A.
Richards's theory of rhetoric as a study of misunderstandings
and their remedies, Booth argues in *The Rhetoric of Rhetoric* for
what he calls "listening rhetoric" rather than "rhetrickery," or
the way rhetoric has come to be commonly known in public
discourse. He creates a taxonomy of rhetoric that includes (1)
win-rhetoric: rhetoric as persuasion and winning at all costs;
(2) bargain-rhetoric: rhetoric as mediation, diplomacy, win-win
rhetoric for both sides; and (3) listening-rhetoric: rhetoric as
a deep probing for common ground. Booth was an optimist
who believed that finding common ground is possible through
listening-rhetoric:

> At its best it [listening-rhetoric] is the quest by the listener
> for some topics, topoi, warrants, to be shared with his or her
> opponent—agreements from which they can move as they probe
> their disagreements. It is the rhetor practicing rhetorology in
> the effort to discover, in the "other," some ground or platform
> where, as a community, they can move from some understanding
> toward some new territory.[64]

Booth's focus on the communal or social nature of rhetorical
agency echoes Burkean identification: "I never think of 'communication' without thinking of its ultimate perfection, named
in such words as 'community' and 'communion.'"[65] For Booth,
rhetoric is an *I* needing to join a *we*.

Other contemporary theories provide valuable ways of thinking about engagements across difference. Linda Flower's theory
for community literacy work and Bruce McComiskey's work on
recovering dialectical elements of rhetoric both have empathetic
threads. Flower synthesizes competing theories for engagement
among critical race theorists and lays out a spectrum of efforts
to engage with difference in her community-literacy work that

provides a useful way of thinking about rhetorical engagement along a spectrum. She writes that "intercultural rhetoric . . . is a place of multiple—and inevitably contradictory—agendas, from self-expression to advocacy to collaborative understanding."[66] Relying on Catherine Prendergast's discussions of critical race theory, Flower defines *self-expression* as an in-group form of resistance and identity formation, the creation of a "special voice" that becomes "the distinctive expression of a postcolonial double consciousness."[67] An example would be using one's own language and not attempting to use the language of the dominant mainstream or even engage with the mainstream.

A second form of resistance that builds on self-expression, a *discourse of disruption,* occurs when a marginalized group protests the mainstream in a way that would be understandable to those outside their own group with the intent to change the mainstream in some way. Flower cites the example of Gwendolyn Pough, who in a 2003 *College Composition and Communication* article describes her activist work at Miami University to highlight the lack of diversity, building on Eric Dyson's work using disruption, intervention, and disturbance.

The third form of engagement, *collaborative understanding,* includes border-crossing rhetoric intended to develop new kinds of knowledge and (thus) formulations of identity and ways of being in the world. Flower cites Jacqueline Jones Royster as an example of wrestling with the tensions of trying to speak in one's own voice and to one's own community and yet trying to be heard by the larger, dominant culture. Flower writes that "without losing the edge of critique, [Royster's] sense of negotiating doesn't seem to depend on the adversarial power moves associated with the discourse of advocacy."[68] Rhetorical empathy resonates with the productive tension Flower describes that "asks people to put aside privileged and/ or familiar ways of talking to one another in order to enter a far less predictable rhetoric of inquiry."[69]

In keeping with rhetorical practices outside the Greco-Roman tradition, McComiskey attempts to integrate elements of dialectic and rhetoric—two strands of ethical reasoning and communicative practices that have operated, for the most part, independently of one another since Aristotle in Western rhetoric. He describes three kinds or dimensions of rhetoric, which he writes are not hierarchical but rather serve different functions:

One-dimensional rhetorics are a single orientation, a self or group talking to others in the group, with the purpose of social unification and coherence. This is the politician (or dictator) trying to "keep his base."

Two-dimensional rhetorics are also a single orientation, talking to or against an opposed orientation. The focus is on power struggles and critique. This is the group defining itself against another group, or identifying itself by what it is against. Two-dimensional rhetorics are, in my view, analogous to Peter Elbow's doubting game, Paul Ricoeur's willingness to suspect, and Eve Sedgwick's notion of paranoid orientation. McComiskey writes that "to belong to a community that is defined oppositionally means be to affected by arguments originating within that community and to be unaffected by arguments originating within opposing communities."[70]

Three-dimensional rhetorics are about mediation and negotiation. According to McComiskey, these kinds of communicative/rhetorical/reasoning styles "require all orientations in any rhetorical situation to be flexible and malleable, and they require all speakers and writers in these same situations to be affectable. . . . There can be no mediation or negotiation among orientations if participants in rhetorical situations are unwilling to be affected by arguments originating from different orientations."[71] Dialectic, when paired with rhetoric, becomes the practice of parties in dialogue to reach a truth, or a way forward in rhetorical terms (in classical Greek terms, dialectic was a way of reaching *the* truth dialogically; that is, through logic by means of dialogue). He associates the emergence of three-dimensional rhetorics with the rise of digital literacies and media. It may seem to go against all evidence to the contrary in our current moment to think about social media being used to find solutions to intractable problems or for people on opposing sides of issues to find ways of engaging with one another on digital platforms. It's not impossible, however, as the examples I underscore in the following chapters suggest.

Feminist Rhetorical Practices: Empathy, Difference, and Embodiment as Ways of Knowing

Empathy-based theories of composition such as Rogerian rhetoric tend to emphasize similarities, connections, and identifications, as have modern theorists of rhetoric and composition such as Richards, Burke, and Booth. Postmodern theories, however, have focused on the embodied subject position, on difference, and on the role of discourse in creating and perpetuating existing power structures (Derrida, Foucault, Fuss). In their emphasis on understanding and finding common ground, modern rhetorical theories have been criticized for simply perpetuating existing power structures that favor people in dominant subject positions (Ratcliffe, Lunsford and Ede, Jarratt, Lassner, Fraser, Benhabib, "Introduction," Mouffe). In modern theories, the minds of interlocutors are, for the most part, disembodied, universal, and decontextualized, much as in the Enlightenment theories of Hume, Adam Smith, and Campbell, which are grounded in psychology. Postmodern, postcolonial, queer, and feminist theories are to a large degree a critique of modern rhetorical theory's lack of attention to the place of the body and difference.

Reframing rhetoric as both an ethical and critical epistemology and practice is (among other things) a feminist project that resists Aristotelian rhetoric and second-problematic thinking described by Hall and Ames. Influential rhetorical theories such as those I've described represent such resistance to varying degrees and have been used, also to varying degrees, for feminist ends—in other words, for the project of identifying and remedying unequal social conditions, especially gender inequities as they relate to other intersectional factors such as race, social class, and labor. A work may not be explicitly feminist in its goals or its original rhetorical context, but following Jarratt's argument in *Rereading the Sophists*, I operate from the premise that a text could be considered feminist in nature based on the rhetorical situation of the text and how it is employed. At the same time, following Gayatri Chakravorty Spivak, just because a text or theory identifies a marginalized Other does not mean it has as its goal the remedying of material conditions for actual women or other marginalized groups.[72]

Beginning with Gertrude Buck in the early twentieth century, feminist rhetorical theories have focused on a more nuanced role of rhetoric as producing greater understanding and a mutual exchange of views. Although women have engaged in public rhetoric for centuries and practiced elements of rhetorical empathy, women's contributions to rhetorical theory began to emerge as late as the early twentieth century in the Euro-American tradition. As women gained access to higher education in the late nineteenth century in greater numbers, they began writing about how to deliver effective speeches and write effective prose rather than exclusively arguing for the right to do so in the public sphere.[73]

The act of women giving speeches and writing for public audiences up to the turn of the twentieth century was news itself. When in 1900 we hear the first sounds of women's voices beginning to break in on the academic scene, it should be no surprise that the perspective we get in Buck's "The Present Status of Rhetorical Theory" is worth noting for its differences from the dominant rhetoric of the time. In an age of theory that had begun to be dominated by myopic concerns with grammar in composition, she wrote about ethics and community and the purpose of rhetoric, arguing a half century earlier than Burke and a century earlier than Booth that when rhetoric is tied to war it becomes a form of manipulation and is not really rhetoric at all. She compared two strains of rhetoric from classical Greece: one she characterized as socially focused on the good of the community and the other as an individually focused form of verbal combat and war, "purely predatory—a primitive aggression of the strong upon the weak."[74] She argues that ethical rhetoric helps "level conditions" between parties and that the

goal of rhetorical exchange should serve the interests of everyone involved.

Sonia Foss and Nancy Griffin in "Beyond Persuasion: A
Proposal for an Invitational Rhetoric" also advocate a peace-
based approach to rhetoric that involves mutual change. They
argue that the definition and function of rhetoric as persuasion is a consequence of "the patriarchal bias that characterizes much of rhetorical theorizing."[75] In response they propose
"an alternative feminist rhetoric" that resists "the traditional
conception of rhetoric . . . characterized by efforts to change
others and thus to gain control over them," rhetoric in which
"self worth [is] derived from and measured by the power
exerted over others, and a devaluation of the life worlds of others . . . , reflecting values of change, competition, and domina-
tion."[76] As in Booth's listening-rhetoric, Foss and Griffin situate rhetoric as an ethical way of negotiating difference rather
than an attempt to win a battle or gain power over others
through manipulation.

Rhetorical empathy builds on such valuable work of feminist theories, based on mutual listening and understanding, the
use of personal narratives, a willingness to yield in a stance of
self-risk and vulnerability, and the celebration of the body and
difference. Groundbreaking work in feminist rhetorical theory
over the past three decades has attempted to disrupt agonistic rhetorics. In their iconic anthology of women's rhetoric,
Available Means, Joy Ritchie and Kate Ronald point to Andrea A.
Lunsford's work *Reclaiming Rhetorica,* in which she writes that we
should not attempt a "new" rhetoric

> but rather . . . interrupt the seamless narrative usually told about
> the rhetorical tradition and . . . open up possibilities for mul-
> tiple rhetorics, rhetorics that would not name and valorize one,
> traditional, competitive, agonistic and linear mode of rhetorical
> discourse but would rather incorporate other, often dangerous
> moves: breaking the silence, naming in personal terms, employ-
> ing dialogics, recognizing and using the power of conversation,
> moving centripetally toward connections and valuing—indeed
> insisting upon—collaboration.[77]

I quote this key passage from Lunsford used by Ritchie and Ronald because its articulation of the goals of feminist rhetorical theories still rings true, and in fact describes the primary underpinnings of this project. In a similar vein, Jacqueline Jones Royster and Gesa E. Kirsch describe a major goal of feminist rhetorical praxis as "learn[ing] to ask new and different questions and find[ing] more and better ways to listen to the multidimensional voices that are speaking from within and across many of the lines that might divide us as language users—by social and political hierarchies, geography, material circumstances, ideologies, time and space."[78] Feminist rhetorical praxis, at its best, both celebrates and negotiates difference.

Another primary feature of feminist rhetoric—some might argue a defining characteristic—is the use of personal, embodied experience in the form of stories that evoke pathos. Influential work such as *Women's Ways of Knowing*, by Mary Field Belenky, Blythe McVicker Clinchy, Nancy Rule Goldberger, and Jill Mattuck Tarule, one of the first books I read in graduate school, opened up the possibility of story as a valid epistemology. Royster and Kirsch write that "we have fashioned our professional identities and laid out paths for research, scholarship, and teaching within this vibrant context [of feminist rhetorical studies], and we have found . . . that stories matter. Consequently, although we might have chosen to introduce this analysis in more-traditional ways, we have chosen instead to begin with our own stories of commitment and connection."[79] I find that reading a bit of a writer's story in a work of scholarship and knowing the personal motivation behind the work usually makes the piece much more interesting and engaging to me.

Linda Adler-Kassner uses a metaphor of a telescope to describe how our personal experience and stories become a lens through which we see the world and larger issues. She connects personal stories to social justice work (the focus of chapter 4 in this book): "Working from our own stories, learning about and connecting with the stories of others—this is the beginning point for building the kinds of alliances that are at the core of story-changing work."[80] Pointing to Parker Palmer's concept

of the undivided self—honoring all parts of our life experience in our teaching, scholarship, and service—she emphasizes
the importance of "working from principle." Our theories, she
holds, rest on the foundation of our principles, without which,
she writes, an argument "literally is academic."[81] Theories work
because they resonate with our own stories and reflect our principles, reminding me of Kate Ronald's adage she often shared
with her graduate students that we shouldn't deny in theory
what we know in our heart to be true.

Feminist theory holds that the personal, the body, and difference are vital factors in decision-making and deliberation.
What if, going back to Hume, our ethical decisions were influenced by how we treat those closest to us? What if we could see
our political Other, whether our coworker, our distant relative
several states removed, or our own father, with the same lens
and thinking and care we reserve for those closest to us? This is
a hard question, and I struggle with it each time I visit my family in Oklahoma and look around at the people sitting in the
diner with me in my parents' small town. Most of them who did
vote cast their ballot for a man in the 2016 presidential election
whose values run counter to everything I believe in—and seemingly to many things they believe in. (Oklahoma had the third-
largest share of Republican voters in the election, just below
Wyoming and West Virginia.) I try to imagine what life is like for
them, and I listen to their stories. I know that if they knew I was
gay they would see me as much more of an outsider than they
already do, though I lived in Oklahoma for almost twenty years
as an adult. I think of Arlie Hochschild's insights in *Strangers in
Their Own Land,* and they resonate, as painful as those insights
are. Hochschild, a self-described liberal academic from Berkeley,
spent five years in southern Louisiana trying to understand the
popularity of the Tea Party movement. Listening to the stories
and spending time with people in a deeply Red state helped her
understand what motivated them to support the Tea Party and,
in turn, to vote as they did in the 2016 presidential election. She
doesn't endorse their decisions, but she describes how listening
and being changed by the emotions that result from listening

opened the way for her to understand the people she met. Her book, which is part academic study and part engaging narrative, goes a long way toward helping people on the Left understand the motives of people and voters on the Right.

Thinking with rhetorical empathy and remembering the stories in Hochchild's work helps me listen. Doing so helps me balance my anger and despair with a realization that if we fail to listen to one another, we simply won't succeed as a democracy. I find myself softening toward the man in the next booth with the red Trump hat, and I sigh. I think of my parents' neighbors in rural Oklahoma, Trump voters who helped care for my mother after she suffered a stroke this year. Would they treat me differently if they knew I was gay? Would they treat anyone who is different from them with respect? I don't know the answer to that, but rhetorical empathy and work such as Hochschild's provide a lens for seeing and listening to people whose social and political views we may profoundly disagree with.

The concept of empathy, unlike its more muscular relative solidarity, suggests an emphasis on the personal. In *Contingency, Irony and Solidarity*, Richard Rorty holds that we have a moral obligation to feel a sense of solidarity with others. Similarly, Jürgen Habermas's notion of solidarity is founded on what Seyla Benhabib calls "the generalized Other," based on the universal principle of respect for all as moral persons.[82] The tradition of ethical formalism emphasizes justice, rights, and universal respect for everyone as moral persons in the tradition of John Stuart Mill's utilitarianism.[83] Habermasian public sphere theory and the notion of the generalized Other emerged from this tradition. In the private sphere is the "concrete Other" and the values of care demanded of us and shown to us by those with whom we are in closest relationship. According to Benhabib, the private sphere is governed by contextual, contingent codes of conduct and is characterized by relationships ideally grounded in empathetic values. Her theory of ethical relationships focuses on public sphere ethics as "preserv[ing] . . . empathy derived from and fostered in small-scale, face-to-face interaction."[84]

Deconstructing the public/private binary, Benhabib points out, has been "one of the chief contributions of feminist thought to political theory in the western tradition." In light of this deconstruction, she imagines an alternative public sphere that includes private morality and feminist voices and concerns.[85] Friedrich Nietzsche, Foucault, and Rorty also argue for a separation of the private sphere from the public in order to (for the most part) protect individual freedom—a reason very different from hers. While acknowledging that Carol Gilligan's theory of moral development has been used against women as a form of essentialism, Benhabib points to the importance of recovering valuable aspects of her theory to formulate new ways of enacting public sphere discourse ethics and theories. She compares the public sphere to Gilligan's *ethic of rights* and the private sphere to her *ethic of responsibility and care.*[86]

Arne Johan Vetlesen resists rationalist, Enlightenment epistemologies, arguing that detachment prevents understanding and that receptivity to others—their perceptions, their emotions, and their motivations—takes the form of empathy.[87] For him, empathy is critical for interpersonal relations to be extended to the public sphere, as in the relation between *I* and *Thou* (Buber, Levinas, Butler), always constituted by difference but also interconnected (Mao, "Returning," Butler, Ratcliffe). Empathy for Vetlesen is a faculty, a cognitive ability, a conscious choice that disposes the subject to develop concern on an emotional level. This concern *changes the subject*; it is not removed from the object at a distance and acting only out of duty or respect for the rights of the object. This definition relates to empathy as feeling *into* rather than sympathy or pity's feeling *for.*

The personal for Vetlesen is political; it involves power, ideology, and language: "At the heart of fostering moral space is a social, indeed a political issue. And politics means power: the power relations at work between people, and often invisible to them, and the forces of repression at work within the individual."[88] Like Hume, Vetlesen argues that empathy is a necessity for morality; he resists a cognitive understanding of moral perception and judgment in the tradition of Immanuel Kant and Habermas.[89] He values "connected" over "detached" epistemologies and emphasizes, as do pragmatists, the importance of experience. He argues that moral (rhetorical) deliberation consists of an interplay of emotional and cognitive components involving perception, judgment, and action. Most relevant to a theory of rhetorical empathy is what happens prior to perception. Connection and embodied experience, including emotions, form our perceptions, and those in turn inform our judgment, which influences our words and actions in a recursive process.

* * *

Almost ten years after Sonia Sotomayor's appointment to the US Supreme Court, it's an understatement to say that empathy still is not popular with (the majority of) Republican politicians. It may seem impossible for values based on the private sphere and empathy to have any bearing on a broken political system. Systems, though, are made up of people and discourse; dominant ideologies can be resisted, as remarkable movements such as Black Lives Matter and #MeToo have shown. In the following chapters, I explore how rhetorical empathy opens avenues for rhetorical engagement across difference in the examples of Jane Addams's embodied, pragmatic rhetoric, in the digital stories of labor activist Joyce Fernandes, in the mediating rhetoric of gay-rights activist Justin Lee, and in writing classrooms.

2

THREADS OF FEMINIST RHETORICAL PRACTICES
Storytelling and Empathy from Gilded Age Chicago to Facebook

Already there is a conviction that we are under a moral obligation in choosing our experiences, since the result of those experiences must ultimately determine our understanding of life. We know instinctively that if we grow contemptuous of our fellows, and consciously limit our intercourse to certain kinds of people whom we have previously decided to respect, we not only tremendously circumscribe our range of life, but limit the scope of our ethics.
— Jane Addams, *Democracy and Social Ethics*

To college students! What's the point in gaining awareness from the stories on this page but then going to your fraternity parties and leaving the place a mess because Monday is "Aunty Cleaning" day? . . . Where's the real empathy?
— Joyce Fernandes, post on the Facebook site "Eu, Empregada Doméstica"

Jane Addams was only thirty-two years old, four years into her work at Hull House, when she delivered a speech on women's working conditions on May 19, 1893, at the World's Columbian Exposition in Chicago.[1] Twenty-seven million people visited Chicago during the exposition, held May 1–October 30, 1893. It spanned six hundred acres, with representatives from forty-six nations taking part. Over two hundred congresses or conferences were held, by far the most popular of which was the Women's Congress, featuring eighty-one sessions and drawing an estimated one hundred and fifty thousand people, mostly women.[2] The congress was an unprecedented platform for women to speak

DOI: 10.7330/9781607329107.c002

publicly on issues of concern to them—the first of its kind in the world. In a small venue reminiscent of an academic conference presentation, a handful of upper-class white women listened to the young Addams, the daughter of a state senator from Illinois who would give up her wealth and social standing to live and work among poor immigrant families in an exploding industrial neighborhood west of downtown Chicago. The experience would change her in ways she could not have comprehended when she first moved into Hull House in 1889. She would go on to found the profession of social work in the United States and was one of the most famous women of her time when she died in 1935, winning the Nobel Peace Prize the year before her death. The stories of the women she worked with changed her and formed her thinking; she relied on them throughout her life to make her arguments for social reform to audiences much like herself: privileged women (and men) who were removed from the suffering of working-class people.

Joyce Fernandes grew up the daughter of a domestic worker in Brazil. She also worked as a maid for seven years before going to college and becoming a history teacher, which she did for five years before pursuing activist work and music full time. Her journey toward becoming a labor- and women's-rights activist began when a media outlet in Sao Paolo featured posts she'd written on her Facebook page in July 2016 about the humiliation she endured in domestic work, as well as growing up black, or *preta*, in Brazilian society. The story was picked up soon after by the BBC, and the social media presence she created to share the stories of other women like herself, "Eu, Empregada Doméstica" ("I, Housemaid"), gained over one hundred thousand followers overnight. She combines her activist work on labor with her well-known persona as a rapper, writing, speaking, and making music focused on racism in Brazilian society and appearing on media as varied as MTV and TED talks. When the BBC circulated her story, she became known beyond Brazil as well.

Fernandes told the BBC that her goal is to "provoke and give voice to the voiceless . . . the majority of whom are black and . . . do not have anyone to vent to." She says she has received thousands of stories, most of which were sent to her by domestic workers' daughters and even granddaughters via email. To date she has posted several hundred of them on the site. She does not post names or images of the women unless they give her permission (and usually she posts only first names).

Both Addams and Fernandes attempt to enact change on a societal level by bringing attention to the very real, personal stories of people caught up in exploitative systems. Both place themselves within the stories they tell: their own experience becomes an important persuasive element in their rhetorical purposes of bringing greater awareness to workers'-rights issues. The comparison I make between the two women hinges not only on their common fight for women's rights and their labor activism but also on their similar rhetorical strategies, separated as they are by over one hundred years and the revolution of digital media and social media networks. Each of them relies on rhetorical strategies I associate with rhetorical empathy:

- Yielding to an Other by sharing and listening to personal stories
- Considering motives behind speech acts and actions
- Engaging in reflection and self-critique
- Addressing difference, power, and embodiment

I have come to see these strategies as core features of feminist rhetorics, especially those focused on listening for and highlighting intersectional power differences. As I suggest throughout this book, rhetorical strategies characterized by a strategic kind of empathy are in keeping with a woman-centered and feminist political philosophy that the personal is always political. Empathy is grounded in pathos and the personal, but it has potential for political power as well. The use of the personal in the form of stories disarms an audience through identification ("You're like me on some level") and so helps bridge gaps in understanding across marked social differences. It's difficult enough to understand our own experiences and motives, but stories invite us to imagine what an Other has gone through in ways other rhetorical appeals cannot.

I imagine rhetorical empathy as both a topos and a trope: a place one chooses to enter to think about how to approach an Other, and discourse and embodied rhetoric characterized by listening and the emotions often associated with such choices to be vulnerable. The tropes and speech acts that result from such a topos are characterized by stories of the Other that resist stereotypes, narratives based on the personal as a way of knowing.[3] Such narratives result from seeing the Other as an individual who is part of a larger system but an individual nonetheless. Personal narratives, a precursor and part of the #MeToo movement, are a defining characteristic of feminist rhetoric and have long been used by women for social change. The use of personal narratives makes both the subject of discourse and the audience or interlocutors within discourse vulnerable in some way, creating an opening for (ex)change. Rhetorical empathy can invoke change because it disarms.

This chapter explores examples of how rhetorical empathy functions in the labor-rights rhetoric of these two complex, compelling women, one hundred years and, in terms of digital technology, light years removed from one another. Both women represent significant milestones for women's speaking out publicly as labor-rights advocates: Addams at the first gathering featuring women's speeches on a global scale at the 1893 World's Columbian Exposition, and Fernandes using the platform of digitized, networked rhetoric on social media with an instantaneous, global reach. I use the characteristics I associate with rhetorical empathy as an organizational framework to look closely at Addams's Columbian Exposition speech and, over one hundred years later, stories of domestic workers Fernandes has curated and brought to international attention.

JANE ADDAMS, FIRST WAVE US FEMINISM, AND WOMEN'S DOMESTIC LABOR

Addams had been invited to speak at a panel at the World's Columbian Exposition on what was beginning to be known as home economics; the respondent to her talk was Mary Hinman

Abel, a pioneer of the movement. It's unknown how many people attended the panel, but other panels at the eight-day, first-of-its-kind World's Congress of Representative Women drew as many as three thousand, including seventy-three-year-old Susan B. Anthony, who spoke the following day advocating for labor unions in the main evening session.

With some exceptions, Addams being the most notable, the most prominent voices for women's rights in the Progressive Era failed to include or represent working-class women. Even otherwise progressive women took for granted the employment of domestic workers and expressed exasperation over the lack of "good servants." In her memoir *Eighty Years and More*, Elizabeth Cady Stanton attributes her discontentment with the conditions of domestic work and the "lack of faithful, competent servants," among other factors, to her involvement with the women's suffrage movement and the Seneca Falls Convention of 1848.[4] Stanton was a featured and honored speaker at the World's Congress of Women, advocating for the rights of women, but the lack of attention among prominent first-wave feminists to the plight of working-class women highlights the degree to which they were focused on women who could claim racial whiteness and who were educated and middle class for the most part.

The push for reform of domestic work had begun twenty-five years before the Columbian Exposition, with the idea of cooperative housekeeping first forwarded in the late 1860s by Melusina Fay Peirce.[5] In Peirce's vision, groups of fifteen to twenty women would form a cooperative designed to aggregate household labor into a collective, relieving individual women/households from the drudgery of domestic labor and replacing unskilled domestic workers with skilled who would run the cooperative. Her idea was deemed too radical and impractical to be implemented on a large scale, requiring large amounts of capital, among other challenges, but another reform idea began to circulate in the early 1890s using capitalist models, namely that of "industrializing" domestic workers, an idea Addams articulates in "A Belated Industry." Charlotte Perkins Gilman, for example, forwards such a model in her novel *What Diantha Did*, focused on leaving domestic work in the hands of individual households but with greater training and organization among domestic workers.

Politically and rhetorically, the speech marks the beginning of an evolutionary process for Addams on labor reform. The panel on which Addams spoke at the Women's Congress was focused not so much on labor reform as on "home economics," appealing to middle-class white women. Addams, however, used the opportunity to advocate for changes in the conditions of working-class women, trying to create awareness of the humanity and living conditions of domestic laborers. In 1898, she would deliver a speech to the General Federation of Women's Clubs in Chicago, making many of the same arguments but also arguing for government intervention. In 1901, she would help form the Working Women's Association of America Union to help improve working conditions and raise wages; and in 1903, Addams and Mary McDowell assisted in founding the first union for female workers on a national scale, the Women's Trade Union League.[6] While Addams would move toward greater government intervention to address social injustices, she maintained her belief throughout her life that true social change could only be accomplished as people were moved in their emotions on a personal level to see the Other as equal within a democracy. She would write in *Twenty Years at Hull House* in 1912 that "social change can only be inaugurated by those who feel the unrighteousness of the contemporary conditions."[7]

Personal Epistemology and Rhetorical Listening: Addams and Hull House

In her Columbian Exposition speech, Addams describes the poor working conditions of domestic workers and portrays them as marginalized members of a democratic society that had become increasingly stratified into classes in the late nineteenth century, a product of the worst aspects of capitalism. Between 1870 and 1902, domestic work was the leading occupation of women; by 1870, one in five Chicago families employed live-in domestic workers, who comprised 60 percent of wage-earning women.[8]

Immigrants and African American women composed the majority of domestic workers prior to 1900 (more than half), with the
number of African Americans rising after World War I. Between
1870 and 1902, domestic work was the leading occupation of
women in Chicago and the nation. Workers usually were young,
single women from working-class families, often newly arrived
Irish, German, Scandinavian, or Polish immigrants in the last half
of the nineteenth century and often among the most desperate
for employment.[9]

While Addams did not formulate a rhetorical theory in a
formal sense, her praxis blurred the lines between theory and
practice. Ritchie and Ronald point out that praxis is "a central
feature of women's rhetorical practices" and that we should
look to praxis as theory.[10] Characteristics of rhetorical empathy appear throughout Addams's public rhetoric, forming
more than a strategy for her; rather, it constituted her embodied identity. Her embodied philosophy/rhetoric of empathy
influenced her engagement with what she called the "common life" of working people at Hull House, resulting in her
use of an empathetic rhetorical style focused on the personal
and solving social problems using cooperative methods.[11] In
crucial ways, Addams's experience at Hull House formed her
epistemological framework. As a pragmatist who held that theory should come from experience, Addams formed her beliefs
as a result of what she experienced firsthand in working-
class neighborhoods.

Addams and her companion Ellen Gates Starr founded Hull
House in 1889 in the working-class nineteenth ward just west
of downtown Chicago. They modeled the settlement house,
the first in the United States,[12] on Toynbee Hall in London,
designed to foster cross-class relationships and "proselytize the
humanities" rather than save souls.[13] Addams's philosophy for
Hull House was that it would provide an opportunity for women
and men with social capital to work alongside residents in
working-class neighborhoods to develop literary, cultural, and
practical skills. Addams tells her audience that her arguments
for worker reform had come from her personal knowledge of

the perspectives of women employed as domestic workers. At the beginning of her speech, she announces that "an attempt is made to present this industry from the point of view of those women who are working in households for wages" and that

> the opinions in [this talk] have been largely gained through experiences in a Woman's Labor Bureau, and through conversations held there with women returning from the "situations," which they had voluntarily relinquished in Chicago households of all grades. These same women seldom gave up a place in a factory, although many of the factory situations involved long hours and hard work.[14]

Her rhetorical style is informed a great deal by her belief in mutual exchange rather than overt persuasion, a belief that undergirded her philosophy at Hull House. Similar to the idea that empathy involves feeling *with* rather than *for* an Other, Addams believed in *being with* people rather than *doing for* them. In this sense she resisted popular, late nineteenth-century notions of the role of what was commonly known as *benevolence*. Rather than trying to persuade people of her own beliefs, Addams tried to forge greater understanding and connection between people in different social classes and ethnic groups. In this process she realized that the greatest good came from gaining the perspective of the Other and that within that learning process, change occurs, both in persuading the Other to accept a new perspective and within the rhetor in listening to the perspective of the Other. Addams's engagement with working-class struggles at Hull House changed her, and her public rhetoric advocating reform was a result of this change.

Pathos and Story Personalizing the Impersonal

Her speech at the Columbian Exposition, though relatively short and obscure, is a good example of her early rhetoric and is representative of her rhetorical style: as in her longer, more well-known work, such as *The Long Road of Woman's Memory*, she relies on her personal experience and on stories to form knowledge and appeal to her audience. In the speech, Addams draws from her friendships and daily interactions with domestic workers at Hull House, using personal stories as emotional appeals to humanize the women most if not all of her audience employed in their homes.

In "Domestic Service" and its fuller version "A Belated Industry," Addams personalizes what had become a considerably impersonal commonplace of middle- and upper-middle-class families employing young women to live full time in their homes as servants. Faye Dudden makes a compelling argument that prior to the 1830s, young women employed by families for domestic work were considered in many cases as part of the family, as "help," eating in the dining room with the other members of the family rather than in a back room or basement and often hired for temporary seasons such as during a family illness.[15] Furthermore, most domestic workers were native-born women whose families lived in the same community as their employers.

Dudden speculates that a shift toward viewing and treating domestic workers as impersonal employees began around midcentury. As industrial capitalism began to take hold, work began to shift away from the home, men began working outside the home, and rising middle-class women began to be seen as the keepers of the home exclusively. In order to preserve "family time" in the evenings, undisturbed by domestic chores such as cleaning and cooking, the woman of the family would hire and supervise one or more servants. Dudden holds that the shift from workers as "help" to "servants" was "demanding and demeaning, prompting the withdrawal from service of many of the native-born daughters who had been willing to help."[16]

The result was an occupation that required young women to live full time with a family, often without any companionship or social outlets, and they were often treated with disrespect or worse by the woman of the house. Dudden points to Gerda Lerner's argument that "the 1830s first saw the lady and the mill girl exemplify the drastically different life courses for women of different classes" and that "the lady's opposite was more apt to be the domestic."[17] Dudden also points out the inherent conflict

between "the triumph of domesticity, of a sentimental association of the hearthstone with the center of the universe and the
foundation of society" and the notion of employing "a strange
woman to sweep up the ashes from it."[18]

In her speech, Addams attempts to humanize the women
working daily in the homes of her audience, focusing on the
isolation it produces in young woman—her primarily argument against the ethically bankrupt system of domestic labor
in her society. She points to the hypocrisy of the women in her
audience who employ young women and require them to live
full time in their homes, denying the women a chance to have
families of their own: "The employer of household labor, in her
zeal to preserve her family life intact and free from intrusion,
acts inconsistently and grants to her cook, for instance, but
once or twice a week such opportunity for untrammeled association with her relatives."[19] She stresses the inconsistencies of
the domestic-labor model with two biting sentences contained
in the Columbian Exposition proceedings (and providing a
memorable impression of Addams) but omitted by Addams or
her editors in the article published in the *American Journal of
Sociology*: "So strongly is the employer imbued with the sanctity
of her own family life that this sacrifice of the cook's family life
seems to her perfectly justifiable. If one chose to be jocose one
might say that it becomes almost a religious devotion, in which
the cook figures as a burnt offering and the kitchen range as the
patriarchal altar."[20]

She describes the changes she's seen in young women after
working as live-in domestics during her time at the Chicago
Labor Bureau: "Many a girl who complains of loneliness, and
who relinquishes her situation with that as her sole excuse,
feebly tries to formulate her sense of restraint and social mal-
adjustment. She sometimes says that she 'feels so unnatural all
the time.'"[21] Addams goes on to point out that

> the writer has known the voice of a girl to change so much dur-
> ing three weeks of "service" that she could not recognize it when
> the girl returned to the bureau. It alternated between the high
> falsetto in which a shy child "speaks a piece," and the husky gulp

with which the *globus hystericus* is swallowed. The alertness and *bon-homie* of the voice of the tenement-house child had totally disappeared.[22]

The young women for whom Addams advocates and whose perspectives she tries to represent in "A Belated Industry" become real people, those living and working in the homes of the women in her audience and suffering under the current system—a system producing bad effects, she argues, not only for domestic workers but for the women who employ them.

Addressing Injustice and Difference: The Personal in the System

Addams's primary argument in her speech is that the domestic-labor system kept alive by the women in her audience suffers from two major flaws: ethical and industrial. In making this argument, she focuses on both the personal and the political. The system of employing young women full time as cooks and housemaids to keep up an antiquated social system deprives, Addams argues, the women of families of their own and isolates them. On a larger level, she points out that her work at Hull House had shown her that the use of such an ethically compromised model drives young women to work in factories, so the best workers are not available for domestic labor. She positions both the women as employers and the young women they employ as human beings, individuals, caught in a larger system that is not good, ultimately, for anyone involved.

The industrial model of live-in housemaids in Addams's argument was part of larger discussions about immigration and capitalism in the mid- to late nineteenth century. A common complaint among middle- and upper-middle-class women was the "lack of good help," a response precipitated in part by the low level of education and the differences in cultural backgrounds of workers, often Catholics serving in Protestant households. Immigrants became scapegoats for what middle-class people thought was wrong with society. In popular publications such as Catharine Esther Beecher and Harriet Beecher Stowe's *The American Woman's Home*, women referred nostalgically to better times in which "mistresses and servants lived together in harmony as equals";[23] Beecher and Stowe argue for a greater sense of egalitarianism among employers and domestic workers in a democratic society. However, the drive toward status and the maintenance of an ideal of domesticity among the growing number of middle-class women virtually required the employment of domestic help. Having a domestic servant who was treated as an equal did not lead to status; in fact, the treatment of domestic workers as Other, as a separate class, was one of the ways people constructed themselves as middle class.

Even though Addams argues in "A Belated Industry" that "it is not the object of this paper to suggest remedies," she suggests to her audience that a good solution to the isolation of live-in domestic workers is to employ them for a regular work day rather than for much of the week except for part of the day Sunday, when they had time off to spend with their friends and families. Such a model would follow the adaptations made in other industries that prior to the industrial revolution were part of a household, such the production and repair of household goods, products, and services that in the late nineteenth century were provided by the shoemaker and the baker on the corner. The idea that such men would be required to live full time with a family, she explains to her audience, is not only unethical but is impractical from an economic standpoint.

She also advocates for the "formation of residence clubs, at least in the suburbs, where the isolation [of domestic workers] is most keenly felt" and providing organized training for domestic workers (which Hull House would eventually do).[24] She concedes that the elimination of such a standard social model as live-in household workers would be a difficult transition for her audience, so she appeals to their identity as "bread givers" to their households, constructing them as morally superior if they took on the work of the household rather than delegating it to a stranger. She concedes that shifting away from employing women as domestic workers, especially as cooks, would drive food production toward the factory model, as had occurred with the production of many household goods within industrial capitalism, a shift that would fall disproportionally to working-class women, which had already happened to a large degree because they did not have time to cook for their own families. She describes an immigrant woman living in a tenement whom she had seen "pass by a basket of green peas at the door of a local grocery store, to purchase a tin of canned peas, because they could be easily prepared for supper and 'the children liked the tinny taste.'"[25]

Addams invites her audience of women who employ domestic help to imagine them as fellow wives and mothers trying to run their own households. She compels her audience to think about how difficult household work is for women who work in factories making the goods the women consume on a daily basis, or who help run the households of women who employ them while also attempting to run their own.

> The difficulties really begin when the family income is so small that but one person can be employed in the household for all these varied functions, and the difficulties increase and grow almost insurmountable as they fall altogether upon the mother of the family, who is living in a flat, or worse still, in a tenement house, where one stove and one set of utensils must be put to all sorts of uses, fit or unfit, making the living room of the family a horror in summer, and perfectly insupportable in rainy washing days in winter.[26]

Unlike Fernandes, Addams never worked as a domestic laborer. She knew women who had and was moved and changed by their stories. Her rhetoric invites the same kind of change in her audience, as they experience someone with whom they can identify—a socially acceptable, upper-class white woman encouraging them to think of the lower-class women in their homes, cleaning up their messes and helping raise their children, as equal to them and worthy of a better life.

TRANSNATIONAL, DIGITAL ACTIVISM: JOYCE FERNANDES, PRETA-RARA, AND "I, HOUSEMAID"

In the hundreds of stories of domestic workers she's posted on the "Eu, Empregada Doméstica" Facebook page, Fernandes humanizes the millions of domestic workers in Brazil who often are invisible or considered unimportant in society because of their occupation or skin color. She shares real women's stories of the abuses they've experienced in their own words—or, because many of the women lack the literacy and access necessary to participate on Facebook, their stories in the words of their daughters and granddaughters. Many of these daughters and granddaughters were themselves domestic workers before going to college; their posts indicate they have internalized the stories of their mothers and grandmothers into their own narratives about the value of their lives and other women of color in their country. The women's stories describe, sometimes in painful detail, the effects of domestic labor—which Fernandes calls "modern-day slavery"—on their physical bodies as well as their self-esteem and ability to have a decent life of their own while taking care of other women in their society.

Fernandes makes it clear that it's just as important to fight the emotional effects of slavery's legacy as it is to fight the legal and material ramifications, resisting the effects of racism in multiple ways. She proudly celebrates her own body and black identity on her professional Facebook page, which she named after her rapper persona, Preta-Rara. She encourages other young black women to see their own worth and advocate for those who still suffer under domestic-labor abuses, and she shares the stories of other domestic workers on the "I, Housemaid" Facebook site. Her performance name is a powerful reclamation of blackness. People with noticeable African features and skin color—those with the darkest skin—are generally referred to as (and they identify as) *negro* or *preto* ("black"). *Preta*, the Portuguese word for "black," is a reclamation similar to the LGBTQ community's reclamation of the term *queer*.[27] *Rara* in the urban dictionary is "lovable" and "the most beautiful and amazing girl ever."[28] Preta-Rara, then, signifies in English something like "queer, wonderful, eccentric black woman." With her assumed name, Fernandes resists racist assumptions and associations of blackness and fights to redefine what it means to be black in Brazil.

She often begins her posts on "I, Housemaid" and her "Preta-Rara" Facebook page—all of which are written in Portuguese and translated into English below—with the salutation "Estamos juntas, Preta-Rara!" ("We are together, Preta-Rara"), so that her stage name becomes a communal name for all women like herself in her culture. In a post on July 25, 2016, just after she created the page on July 21 and it went viral with worldwide media coverage, she describes the purpose for the site, using the third-person, communal plural to speak on behalf of other women like herself:

> We are together, Preta-Rara!
>
> Since Thursday, July 21, the hashtag #EuEmpregadaDoméstica (via social media) made us think about the place reserved for black women in this society. . . . They take care of the sons of others . . . and in most cases receive a low salary. In addition, there are no labor rights such as vacations, annual bonuses, payments for night shifts, overtime, health insurance, transportation vouchers and food stamps. And this reminded us (no big news) of the low position of this job, not being allowed to access living spaces in their own place of employment, not being able to take the main elevator, sit at the table for meals, and eating meals that are different from those of their bosses.

She goes on in the same post to address and resist the low position of black women in Brazil: "And even when we develop or when we insist on leaving these jobs, they intend to point out that the large population of black women—at the base of the social pyramid—should remain there."

Despite the well-earned criticism Facebook has received for its role in promoting political division during the 2016 election in the United States, and for its lack of transparency in describing to users how their information will be used (and sold), the fact is that without Facebook, the stories of these women would, in all likelihood, not be told, at least not on the level afforded by social media. Many posts receive several hundred comments, some from people pushing back against her message, expressing disbelief at what she's writing, and many offering support and writing their own messages about family members or friends. The circulatory reach of these posts is multiplied within Facebook's algorithm, which allows users to view comments made by their friends, exposing the women's stories to the social network of the tens of thousands of people who follow her feed. Considering how these posts and stories "travel" and are dispersed among varied networks and audiences, using frames such as circulation and mobility studies is useful in thinking about the role of online networks in social change. The concept of circulation—what Laurie E. Gries describes as a key threshold concept for rhetorical studies—alongside a lens of rhetorical empathy provides useful ways of thinking about audience and affect in digital spaces.[29]

Her many audiences include not only other women like herself, whom she encourages to advocate for others still in domestic work and shut off from opportunities despite the improvement of labor laws, but also young women in college who are fans of her music. In a post on her Facebook page on October 22, 2016, she writes,

> To college students!
> What's the point in gaining awareness from the stories on this page but then going to your fraternity parties and leaving the place a mess because Monday is "Aunty Cleaning" day? And beyond the everyday mess, she is forced to collect cans, used condoms, empty loaded ashtrays, and face the bathroom just as you can imagine right now, and still she's paid R$ 50 for the job. Rethink your life and your ideas, get off the Internet and seek change for the world that you always talk about. Where's the real empathy?

This post highlights Fernandes's use of her music platform and status as a rap star to reach audiences who may never be exposed to or interested in labor issues for domestic workers. She asks her audience to try to imagine what life is like for the women who clean up after them in their dorm rooms and apartments while they're partying and going about their lives. The affective power of this post, of course, lies in the fact that she herself has been both the college student and the woman cleaning up, so to speak.

Her story represents one of millions of women in Brazil working as domestic maids, a position typically filled by women

of color as a vestige of legalized slavery and a result of staggering income inequality. US media coverage of the 2016 Summer
Olympics in Rio de Janeiro glossed over or failed entirely to
account for the country's income inequality and crime that
are intricately tied to its history of slavery and continued racism. Media images focused instead on the result of this history,
portraying the city as plagued by crime and pollution, with the
Olympic City standing as a staged, security-filled semimirage.
Young, dark-skinned boys, shirtless, ran among tourists in city
squares, captured on surveillance footage attempting to pick-
pocket tourists in the city for the games. US Olympic swimmer
Ryan Lochte made up a story about being robbed at gunpoint
by locals to cover up a night of drunken vandalism.[30] One of the
stories behind Lochte's fictionalized crime runs deep. Of the
eleven million people brought to the Americas in the Middle
Passage, four million ended up in Brazil in its three hundred-
year history of slavery that ended in 1888.[31] These staggering
numbers make the country "the second blackest nation in the
world" after Nigeria, according to Henry Louis Gates Jr.[32]

As in the United States, the racism and exploitation that
drove slavery in Brazil still exist today. The income and wealth
gap between those coded white and those coded nonwhite
is staggering: nonwhite people earn only 60 percent of what
whites earn, which is 84 percent of total income.[33] Women of
color in Brazil traditionally have worked in disproportionate
numbers as domestic laborers, which has roots in legalized slavery. Sandra Lauderdale Graham points out that "in the 1870s,
87–90% of slave women in Rio worked as domestic servants, and
an estimated 34,000 slave and free women labored as domestics.
Thus, Brazilian women in urban centers often blurred the lines
that separated the work and lives of the slave and the free."[34]
Today Brazil has the largest number of domestic workers in
the world at six million,[35] almost one in every five women in
the country, the majority of whom are black women with little
education.[36]

The hundreds of posts on "Eu, Empregada Doméstica"
contain story after story about physical and psychological

trauma faced by women in domestic work, often as a result of the lack of maternity leave or other basic rights enjoyed by most other workers. The stories on the site describe the isolation—pointed to by Addams—of young women cut off from normal family life and subjected to almost unspeakable horror in some cases. On August 3, 2016, Fernandes posted a harrowing story sent by a woman whose mother was a domestic worker for decades.

> My mom has been a maid for 40 years and here is the story that left her terrified:
> In 1989 I was two years old and it was typical for maids with children to live in their employer's house. One day my mother's boss offered to buy me because she couldn't get pregnant, and claimed that my mom wouldn't have resources to take good care of a child, being a single mother. She must have thought that my mother would accept it just like the other maid did, and the worst thing was that the child's mother was still working in the house and kept seeing her son calling another woman mother. My mom got scared and left in the middle of the night.

Another post from October 12, 2016, highlights the lack of maternity leave for household workers in Brazil, which causes many women to work right up until giving birth.

> My mother's dream was to host a big party for her first daughter's one-year birthday. She said she did the cleaning every day to pay her debts and save some money for that long-awaited day. During her pregnancy, I was almost born inside the house where she worked, because just like it is today, she had an informal employment and no right to maternity leave. All her efforts led to a beautiful party that was only possible on my second birthday.
> Mom, thank you for all the effort and dedication, for all the humiliation that you suffered to be able to help dad with the household expenses and raise four children. Doing the cleaning being pregnant and heavy is an absurd and a gross disrespect to women, and so she worked during her three pregnancies, always up to the 9th month. I stand up to it because you do as well, and give me strength to go on every day. Mrs. Helena, you are a Queen.

Other stories recount women who were denied water so they would not have to relieve themselves, older women who were

forced to take the stairs to upper floors when the service eleva-
tor was out and they were barred from using the main eleva-
tor, and women forced to eat on the floor rather than sit at the
table with the family while they ate. The emotions these stories
elicit, both in the writers of the comments on the posts as well
as countless more who read and do not post, create a sense of
empathy with women caught in a system with little protection
from the legal system and little respect in society.

Fernandes resists the idea that domestic work is necessary,
though she is realistic in her doubts about its elimination, often
using humor as well as showing a great deal of emotion in her
writing and live performances and speeches (including a TEDx
Talk in Sao Paulo in November 2016). On July 21, 2016, the
day she launched "I, Housemaid" on Facebook, she questioned
the necessity of domestic labor on the scale it currently exists
in Brazil: "From the G1 piece [a media outlet that first featured
her story], 'If we can clean our own bodies, why can't we clean
our garbage? Why do we need maids?' I'm here to tease, let's
talk about it! And our voice echoes."

Characteristic of empathetic rhetorical practices, she focuses
on the personal within the systemic; she listens and invites listening and its attendant emotion and calls for social change. In the
stories she shares on the site, she describes in poignant detail
the many abuses by employers of domestic workers, but she also
resists painting such people as entirely bad, characterizing them
rather as part of a larger, racist culture. In one of her first posts
(July 21, 2016), she describes how she left domestic work and
went to college. The post on one hand reads almost like a coded
literacy narrative meant to appeal to Left-minded, middle- and
upper-class women who employ domestic workers. However, by
the end of the story, there is a sense that she is being sincere: she
appreciates and even cares deeply for the woman she worked for.
She offers a picture that goes against the stereotypes that easily
could be constructed by her efforts in telling the women's stories
and in doing so offers an affective appeal, consciously or not, to
other women who employ domestic workers.

BOSS: Joyce, I see you taking so long to dust off the shelf and my books, do you like reading?

ME: Yes, I read the Bible a lot.

BOSS: I have already caught you hiding and reading my book "Olga." You can take it home to read. Have you ever considered continuing your studies?

ME: Yes, I want to go to college to study history; it's very expensive, and I don't know if I can afford it.

BOSS: That's amazing, you will have to read a lot, huh! And you will have a shelf with far more books than the lawyer here. You will get it girl, I'm sure. (My boss Regina is the only one who encouraged me to study, and when I met her at Gonzaga beach in Santos/SP, I gave her a big hug and said that I was a teacher, and we cried together).

A number of the women who post responses to the women's stories on "I, Housemaid" appear from their avatars and rhetoric to be well-educated allies of Fernandes's work, so an attempt to reach out to them as shapers of public opinion and policy among the powerful white ruling class makes sense. It's important to stress, however, that Fernandes mixes her graciousness with a great deal of sarcasm, and with anger and confrontation, highlighting injustices, extreme power, and income inequality in her country and their daily consequences. A July 24, 2016, post reads,

The G1 website published a story on the "I, Maid" webpage three days ago.

They talked about the campaign I created and posted a random photo from Facebook, where I'm wearing blue lipstick, sunglasses, and with my black hair up high, reflecting my self-esteem. There were so many racist comments, trying to offend my race, that G1 disabled the comment option at the end of the article.

The Master's House freaked out! We lifted the carpets and showed the dirt and scum that the traditional Brazilian family has been hiding indoors for centuries. That's it! I left a place where many others have left before me, many of them leaving with me, and several ones that will leave soon, because our voice now echoes in the world. And you, sucker racists, won't stop me! AND I'M NOT ALONE, AND HAVE NEVER BEEN! I have several Black Women with me, standing up to it every day and willing to show up, because we are tired of being invisible in this racist society!

Both Fernandes and Addams compel their audiences to view domestic workers as individuals with lives and histories of their own. Addams uses rhetorical empathy to appeal to her audience of middle- and upper-middle-class white women to change the way they approach the issue of immigrant women working in undesirable conditions as maids and cooks in their homes. Fernandes also' uses elements of rhetorical empathy in the form of stories that arouse emotion in her audiences. Fernandes's experience as a domestic worker enables her to approach her audience of other young women like herself and women who employ domestic workers as one who knows intimately about the suffering and journeys she writes about. This additional element of her subject position and experience adds power to her rhetorical appeal based on personal experience.

In Fernandes's words, both women attempt to "humanize the relationship between employers and employees," Addams in the genre of the public speech, commonly used by women in the late nineteenth-century United States, and Fernandes in digital environments of much greater scope than Progressive Era print media environments.[37] Digital social media provides a circulatory power and rhetorical velocity for Fernandes's rhetoric and activist efforts that Addams could not imagine (though it's interesting to think about how she would function in contemporary media culture).[38] The fact that viewers can "scan" quickly through these digital stories in a passive, voyeuristic consumption of the Other could arguably contribute to the disintegration of empathy and social connection, as Sherry Turkle argues in *Reclaiming Conversation*.[39] However, the presence of a discursive community writing their emotions and reactions to the stories and posts on "Eu, Empregada Doméstica" creates a participatory, communal aspect that facilitates empathetic responses. The participatory writing on social media opens a space that is enhanced rather than diminished by its dispersed circulation in digital spaces. Further, social media's reach facilitates a communal experience around shared trauma.

Fernandes also represents a significant shift within intersectional, transnational women's rhetorical practices: from one relying primarily on women in privileged positions speaking for migrant women and women of color without class privilege to women of color in postcolonial contexts gaining access to cultural capital through traditional and digital literacy and advocating themselves for change in attitudes, practices, and public policy.

3
RHETORICAL EMPATHY IN THE GAY-RIGHTS/RELIGIOUS DIVIDE

When a conflict implicates issues of identity . . . there may be a greater tendency towards framing issues in moral terms. Once a dispute is framed in [these] terms, identity is often defined in opposition to "the other."

—Jennifer Gerarda Brown, "Peacemaking in the Culture War Between Gay Rights and Religious Liberty"

My approach is to be vulnerable and let people get to know me for who I am, not who they might have imagined me to be. Once we see each other as fellow human beings and not as stand-ins for sides in a culture war, we can begin the conversation about how we disagree and why.

—Justin Lee

The full inclusion of LGBTQ people in society has been one of the most polarizing issues in conservative religious communities in recent years. In this chapter I analyze how rhetorical empathy functions in an important and kairotic site of civil rights struggles—the intersection of gay rights and conservative Christian discourse—providing a unique examination of ways insiders within one of the more conservative segments of Christianity engage antigay rhetoric in their own community. I analyze an extended online exchange about sexuality and religion between gay-rights activist Justin Lee and an audience of mostly evangelical Christians. The exchange, titled "Ask a Gay Christian," was part of a series of blog posts on what were considered controversial topics to evangelical audiences on the website of the late Rachel Held Evans, an influential blogger and best-selling author. Before her untimely death at thirty-seven on May 4, 2019, Held Evans maintained an active website where she explored

DOI: 10.7330/9781607329107.c003

controversial topics within conservative Christianity and advocated for marginalized groups in the church.[1]

As she had done in other exchanges, in a post on the "Ask a . . ." series on September 13, 2011, Held Evans began the exchange by asking her readers to post questions for Lee and then vetted the top questions based on the number of "likes" a question received. Held Evans posted Lee's discursive responses to the questions on her website the following week. My analysis centers on the ten questions Lee received from her audience and his discursive interactions with readers in the question-and-answer process and is supplemented by Lee's reflections on his rhetorical strategies I gained from an interview with him. I focus on this example of Lee's rhetoric because, unlike his book, the exchange in which he participates on Held Evans's website provides insight into how an audience reacts to his rhetoric; it's an exchange rather than a monologue.

Frequent readers of Held Evans's website were accustomed to an atmosphere of civil discourse, regardless of how divisive or heated a topic may have been. Held Evans set a tone on her site and within the "Ask a . . ." series that invited civil exchange. She established a normative framework for rhetorical exchanges with the following blurb in her comment section: "Please remember the point of our interview series is not to debate or challenge, but to ask the sort of questions that will help us understand one another better. I'll be monitoring the comment section to make sure the questions are civil and fair." It's not possible to determine how many comments she deleted from the exchange, but the majority of comments were civil if not explicitly supportive of Lee, even if the poster disagreed with him, which I discuss below. While I focus on Lee's rhetoric in this particular exchange and blog post, Held Evans's own rhetorical style deserves much credit for the degree of empathy demonstrated by interlocutors on her website.

Lee is a prominent voice in the United States on the intersection of sexuality and religion, especially within efforts to bridge LGBTQ and conservative, evangelical communities. He speaks in venues across the US, particularly college campuses and churches, on the issue of religion and sexual orientation. He's the author of two books, *Talking Across the Divide: How to Communicate with People You Disagree With* and *Torn: Rescuing the Gospel from the Gays Vs. Christians Debate.* In 2009 he directed the documentary "Through My Eyes" about gay youth in Christian churches. He has appeared in media such as CNN, National Public Radio, and the *New York Times.*

Lee's upbringing in the Southern Baptist religious tradition and his coming out as a gay man in his late teens played major roles in his ability to speak with credibility to Christian audiences who are antigay or questioning their long-held commonplaces surrounding homosexuality. Rather than leave his faith tradition, as many LGBTQ-identified people choose or are forced to do, Lee formed the Gay Christian Network in 2001, a national support network for people in his position: Christians who identify as LGBTQ and do not wish to abandon their faith. His activism within evangelical Christian discourse communities takes a more subtle form than more direct, confrontational approaches associated with mainstream gay-rights activists (such as journalist and blogger Dan Savage), who critique antigay rhetoric in the church from an outsider position.

My arguments about the function of rhetorical empathy in this site contribute to Crowley's exploration of ways progressives can engage with fundamentalist Christian rhetoric in *Toward a Civil Discourse: Rhetoric and Fundamentalism.* She argues that fundamentalism relies on a closed system that is not open to logical arguments; like progressivism, it relies on a complex system of interwoven beliefs she calls "ideologics"—patriarchy and homophobia, for example—and that untangling one facet often leads to an entire belief system changing.[2] She points out that the kind of transformation involved in fundamentalists changing their minds on issues of significance usually does not involve logical arguments but rather a crisis or a shift in who holds credibility in a person's life.[3]

Rhetorical empathy as an explanatory theory attempts to account for the emotional component of empathy that can result when the Other becomes a real human being with a face and a family and motivations behind their actions and words. Crowley touches on the personal element of rhetoric and of proximity as a motive for change when she relates a story in Stanley Fish's *The Trouble with Principle*. A Klansman changes his views after he hears a Klan leader say that when the Klan gained ultimate power in society, "Defectives of a variety of kinds would be put into special colonies or otherwise dealt with."[4] He changes his beliefs when he realizes a condition his own daughter suffers with is included among those on the list. Research has shown that when people actually know someone who is lesbian, gay, or bisexual, support for marriage rights for LGBTQ people rises significantly. According to the Public Religion Research Institute,

> Among Americans with a gay or lesbian close friend or family member, seven in ten (70 percent) support same-sex marriage, compared to fewer than half (42 percent) of those without a friend or relative who is gay or lesbian. Although a slim majority (51 percent) of Republicans *oppose* same-sex marriage, a majority (57 percent) of Republicans who report having a gay or lesbian friend or family member *support* same-sex marriage.[5]

Building on the personal element involved in persuasion, Crowley points out that outsiders to the faith have difficulty engaging with insiders on polarizing topics. Her focus on finding ways toward a more civil discourse among polarized groups should, according to her own admission, focus on firsthand, experiential knowledge and ways subalterns within religious discourse communities can gain access to the power required to shift deeply held ideologies.[6] The likelihood that outsiders to conservative religious discourse communities will hold sway against densely held belief systems is quite small, considering the degree to which such belief systems are closed to outside influences. She argues that change in such systems usually happens through those in subaltern subject positions rather than those who enjoy the most privilege in a group: "Their interpretations [of their belief] can never be gainsaid by outsiders, who are agents of evil. They can, however, be questioned by insiders who for some reason experience the subaltern or double consciousness, when, for example, their experience does not square with what they are being taught."[7] Lee functions as both an insider and an outsider to the community he engages with in the exchanges I discuss: he is an insider in that he continues to identify as an evangelical Christian, yet he is an outsider to mainstream evangelical culture, which, as I have noted, remains firmly antigay in its ideology and rhetoric.

I focus on the intersection of gay rights and conservative Christian rhetoric in particular for a number of reasons. First, despite increased acceptance of same-sex relationships, LGBTQ equality remains one of the most polarizing civil rights struggles in the United States. While broad gains for gay people have occurred in recent years—the Windsor Supreme Court case granted marriage rights to LGBTQ people in the United States, and a majority of people nationwide express support for gay marriage rights—a great deal remains to be done to ensure LGBTQ people have equal protections under the law. The presidential election of 2016 and conservative appointments to the US Supreme Court potentially could reverse years of gains for LGBTQ people.

Second, resistance to same-sex relationships remains most pronounced among people identifying as conservative Christians. Since the rise of the gay-rights movement in the 1970s and with the rise of groups in the United States such as the Moral Majority around the same time, the religious right has consistently used the strategy of pitting gay people against people of faith in the United States, constructing LGBTQ people as antireligious "sinners." Among those most against acceptance of gay rights are white evangelical Protestants in the United States. In March 2017, the Public Religion Research Institute reported that a majority of people in the United States (63 percent) favor the right of lesbians and gay men to marry. White evangelical Protestants, however (the focus of this chapter), are the most vocal group opposed to LGBTQ rights in the country, with only 34 percent supporting same-sex marriage.[8] After the defeat of Proposition 8 in California in November 2008, prominent gay-rights groups in the United States such as the

Gay and Lesbian Alliance Against Defamation (GLAAD), the Human Rights Campaign, and gay publications such as *LGBTQ Nation* increased their focus on highlighting the role of faith in LGBTQ people's lives.

Third, I focus on rhetorical strategies within the site of gay-rights and religious rhetoric because many of our students come from religious backgrounds, are LGBTQ, or both and because statistics indicate many of those students refuse to abandon their faith tradition in order to claim an authenticity in their relationships. As a Barna Group study released in 2009 found, 70 percent of LGBTQ adults self-identify as Christian, and 60 percent as "born-again Christians," a moniker often associated with evangelical Christians. George Barna, himself a conservative-leaning evangelical, said of the survey results, "People who portray gay adults as godless, hedonistic, Christian bashers are not working with the facts. A substantial majority of gays cite their faith as a central facet of their life, consider themselves to be Christian, and claim to have some type of meaningful personal commitment to Jesus Christ active in their life today." In *College English*, T. J. Geiger asks teachers and scholars in rhetorical studies to consider effective ways of negotiating the intersections of sexuality and religion in our pedagogy, arguing that "the interpenetrating discourses of religion and sexuality saturate ideological formations, inform individual and community lives, and shape persuasive possibilities."[9] The arguments I make about the value of rhetorical empathy in the public venues I highlight in this chapter hold value for our pedagogy and our students as well.

In what follows, I analyze Lee's rhetorical strategies using the characteristics and recursive practices I associate with rhetorical empathy:

- Yielding to an Other by sharing and listening to personal stories
- Considering motives behind speech acts and actions
- Engaging in reflection and self-critique
- Addressing difference, power, and embodiment

I analyze ways in which all four strategies function in Lee's rhetoric, emphasizing their recursive, interrelated characteristics using examples from the blog post itself, as well as analyzing transcripts from my interview with him about his rhetorical strategies.

THE PERSONAL WITHIN DISCOURSE SYSTEMS: LISTENING TO STORIES

Lee uses rhetorical empathy and its emotion-based appeals grounded in personal experience to connect with his audience and challenge their commonplaces about LGBTQ people. He emphasizes his experience as a former, well-meaning, antigay Christian to identify with those in his audience who hold the same views. By extending empathy to his audience rather than judging them and by avoiding theoretical, scriptural arguments, he places the focus on personal experience and creates an empathetic response from his audience in turn. In his responses to the questions in the "Ask a Gay Christian" exchange, Lee emphasizes his experience as a devout evangelical who once doubted whether identifying as both gay and religious was possible. He identifies with his audience by establishing his credibility as an insider of their community, writing, "I grew up in a loving Christian home, accepted Christ at a young age, attended a Southern Baptist church, and generally had a pretty awesome upbringing. . . . I got the nickname 'God Boy' in high school because I was the Bible-toting goody two-shoes Christian who didn't smoke, drink, curse, have sex, or shut up about God!"[10]

After constructing himself as the kind of evangelical Christian that even the most devout person in the audience would respect and by setting himself up as a stereotype using humor and disarming his audience, Lee expresses his views about being gay before he came out and reconciled his faith and sexual orientation. In the process he addresses lines of argument familiar to his audience.

> My view of homosexuality was this: God created male and female for each other. Our bodies were designed to fit together in that way, and the Bible made it clear that while sexuality was a

gift from God, using our sexuality in ways that were outside of God's design for it was a sin—whether that meant premarital sex, adultery, or homosexuality. My pro-gay friends called me a "homophobe" for this view, but I didn't hate or fear gay people; I simply believed that they were making a sinful choice with their lives, and that by speaking out in a loving way, I could call their attention to it and help bring them back to God.[11]

He disarms his audience by constructing himself as genuine in his religious faith and as having the sincerely held belief he was doing the morally right thing by standing up for his beliefs in rejecting homosexuality. Just as he did not, his audience does not consider themselves haters or homophobes but are doing what they believe to be morally required of them by their faith. He carefully creates a story that draws his audience in rather than alienating them, and in the process he attempts to build his credibility by focusing on his identity as a fellow believer rather than the stereotype of LGBTQ people as antireligious. In doing so he resists the binary of Christian and gay, instead weaving a narrative that combines his two identities and constructs a line of reasoning that becomes difficult for his audience to argue with.

He appeals to his audience's emotions by sharing his coming-out story and pointing out that he was sincerely wrong about homosexuality when he admitted to himself he was attracted to men.

I, of course, wasn't gay. At least, that's what I thought. But I did have a secret I was going to take to my grave. . . . Even if I could make it through the school day without thinking about guys, I'd go to bed at night and dream about guys. I'd wake up each morning feeling dirty and disgusted with myself. As you might expect, I was *horrified* by this. I couldn't tell anyone, and I didn't know what was wrong with me. It got to the point that I was crying myself to sleep, night after night, begging God to take away these feelings. It wasn't until I was 18 (and dating a beautiful girl I had no attraction to whatsoever) that I finally realized there was a word for people like me: "gay."[12]

Lee performs rhetorical empathy in this passage on a number of levels. He foregrounds his body and the ways he's different from his audience in terms of his sexuality, building on and juxtaposing the identifications with them he has established thus far. He elicits an emotional response to his experience of realizing his identity as a gay man directly contradicted the teachings of the church he'd been exposed to since birth. Finally, emphasizing that he tried to fight his feelings, he identifies with the commonplace among evangelicals that homosexuality should be resisted regardless of its origins—genetic, environmental, or otherwise.

He ends his narrative by inviting his audience to identify with him further: imagine, he implicitly asks, if you were trying to fight something you'd been taught was wrong and your religious community rejected you for doing so. His narrative constructs a no-win situation for LGBTQ people within the conservative church.

> As I turned to my church and the Christians I respected most to get their support, things only got worse. Christian groups kicked me out or turned their backs on me when they learned I was gay, even though I told them I didn't want to be and that I hadn't even acted on my feelings! I learned that that one magic word, "gay," had the power to make Christians turn unkind and uncompassionate without even realizing they were doing it.[13]

He invites his audience to listen to his story as both similar and different from their own: they all have struggles, he implies. What if they were rejected for doing what they thought was the right thing? How have they done the very same thing to LGBTQ people they know, even though they may have thought they were acting morally at the time? He performs rhetorical empathy by sharing his story, identifying with his audience, and assuming good motives for them, and he solicits empathy from them in turn by appealing to his credibility as a fellow believer and to their emotions as they realize he was unfairly stigmatized by people who espouse loving even one's enemies yet couldn't love their own.

Lee also uses rhetorical empathy to tackle his most formidable constraint and the commonplace that dominates his audience's thinking: the several passages in the Christian scriptures that supposedly condemn homosexuality. Rather than debating the biblical verses with his questioners, his strategy is to share his own experience. He tells them that despite his sincere efforts to do what was required of him in the teachings of his church, he could not change his attraction to men. After he argues for the hard-wired nature of sexual orientation by sharing his story, he uses emotional appeals by inviting his audience to imagine what it would be like to have to live without their spouse or without love for the rest of their lives: "Once I discovered that it was unlikely I would ever become attracted to women, I realized with despair that this meant I would have to be celibate and alone for the rest of my life. I was willing to do it if that was God's call for me, but the idea of being alone my whole life was a scary, sobering thought. Some people deal well with that; I'm not one of those people."[14]

During this narrative he goes from being a devout evangelical believer (like his audience), to realizing he is gay and being rejected by his church (soliciting his audience's emotions), to becoming an advocate for justice and working toward full equality for LGBTQ people in the conservative church.

When I asked him to talk about his strategy of identifying with his audience through the use of stories and personal appeals, he discussed his motivations and the responses he often gets from such an approach.

> Overall, I find that [using stories] is usually really successful at changing the tone of the conversation and getting people to think more deeply, which is what I really care about. There are always some folks who only want a debate, and some who seem to ignore the content of my response and only focus on their pre-conceived image of me, but I find that most people respond really well. I frequently hear from people who tell me that a conversation we had months or even years earlier was instrumental in helping them rethink the issues and grow closer to an LGBTQ family member or friend.[15]

CONSIDERING MOTIVES BEHIND SPEECH ACTS AND ACTIONS

In addition to using emotional appeals and personal experience, in this exchange Lee keeps in mind the motives—the hopes and fears and social positioning—of his audience, avoiding trigger words that may alienate them and eliminate the chance they will listen to him. Jean Decety and Meghan Meyer point to the complexity of empathy and the role of motives in empathetic responses.

> Empathy is a complex construct and [our] model does not account for all that empathy entails. The phenomenological experience of empathy and its role in initiating prosocial, empathic reactions likely draws on several interacting factors (and complicated distributed brain networks) not mentioned in our review. For example, motivation likely influences empathic accuracy: people who are motivated to produce empathically accurate responses to another's predicament are less susceptible to social inference biases such as the fundamental attribution error (Fletcher, Reeder, & Bull, 1990; Tetlock, 1985).[16]

As Decety and Meyer point out, empathy is complex, and one of the mitigating factors not covered in their study on empathy within the field of psychology is that motives play a role in how empathy functions—certainly pointing toward implications for rhetorical theory that can bear on increasingly complex cross-disciplinary theories on empathy. Adler-Kassner points to the importance of examining what she calls our own and others' "principles" (and which I conceive as similar to motives and Stephen Toulmin's warrants). She points out that our principles arise from and give rise to our stories and that we must attempt to understand the sources of people's anger—or love.[17]

Our lack of understanding of the motives of the Other often fuels our decision not to identify, let alone empathize. Burke points out that identifications are associated with ethics, motives, and irrational elements in human relations. His theory of dramatism in *A Grammar of Motives* attempts to ascertain motives of agents in communicative acts (of the five components of his dramatistic pentad—act, scene, agent, agency, and purpose—the latter asks *why* the agent acted as they did and *what the agent wants* from the rhetorical act). While it's impossible to separate the personal from the public or to claim agency apart from the discourses and *habitus* from which we are formed and in which we operate from moment to moment, Lee's rhetorical strategies suggest that attempting to understand the motives of an Other provides a degree of rhetorical agency and perspective. It's important to stress the *attempt* to understand motives, or, as Lynch puts it, the attempt to *approximate* empathy. While it's often difficult to understand our own motives much of the time, let alone those of others, we can, by using an epistemological lens of rhetorical empathy, choose to have what Addams called an "affectionate interpretation" of someone's intentions.[18]

In "Peacemaking in the Culture War Between Gay Rights and Religious Liberty," Jennifer Gerarda Brown argues for the value of considering motives and the Other's point of view in legal mediation cases involving (perceived and real) clashes between gay rights and religious liberties, cases that often have no long-term winners. She points to psychological theories such as attribution error to explain why polarization occurs over what are perceived as moral issues.

> While we usually assume that people can control their own dispositional characteristics, situational characteristics stem from conditions that are not chosen and give rise to "consequences . . . beyond the actor's control." Thus, in many negative situations, a person who has suffered harm makes an interpretive choice: will she see the harm as (1) the result of qualities, characteristics, and choices within another person's control, (2) the unintended consequence of factors beyond another person's control, or (3) some combination of the two? This interpretive choice has a significant effect on the conflict because it can so directly affect emotions. Russell Korobkin observes that "feelings of being disrespected, demeaned, or otherwise treated unfairly," that would so naturally arise from tangible harm within someone else's control, would be far less likely to flow from harm that appears "beyond the harmdoer's control."[19]

Lee's rhetoric points to the importance of being able to see the lack of agency within someone's actions and words despite the fact that those words and actions may be highly injurious, immoral, and worth condemnation. His example also suggests that an approach based on empathy is within the ability of those in nondominant subject positions to adopt, despite an otherwise lack of agency and power within discursive situations in everyday life and in larger institutional and cultural contexts.

The issue of identity is intricately interwoven into motives and identification to the degree that even engaging with the "other side" can be perceived as a foundational threat to self- and group identity in some cases, as Brown discusses.

> When a conflict implicates issues of identity . . . there may be a greater tendency towards framing issues in moral terms. . . . Once a dispute is framed in moral terms, identity is often defined in opposition to "the other." Thus, identity and moral indignation fall into a reinforcing loop. Making a concession—even in the form of entering into a negotiation—may be seen not only as a moral concession, but even as a potential threat to one's identity.[20]

This threat to identity is often apparent in the discourse surrounding gay rights and religious liberties. If, for example, someone on the side of LGBTQ equality uses a term like *homophobe*, *bigot*, or *hater*, such a move may immediately cut off any chance of engagement with someone invested in protecting what they see as tradition and standing up for the tenets of their faith. Lee deliberately avoids using trigger words and thus alienating his audience by making them feel as if he's attacking their character. Brown points to the importance of separating identity or character and tangible circumstances and material interests in specific rhetorical situations.

> One of the hallmarks of mediation is that, when it is done well, it challenges parties in conflict to get behind and beyond labels like "bigot" and unpack phrases like "homosexual agenda." The rhetorical devices that some activists on both sides use to stir the ground troops may be absorbed and internalized by individuals who find themselves in actual, concrete conflicts—but those rhetorical devices are often singularly unhelpful in actually resolving the conflicts. Mediation can help the parties acknowledge "the degree to which material and tangible interests (as opposed to 'morality' or character) are determining the behavior of both sides."[21]

Lee's empathetic approach has a great deal of rhetorical significance because of his own positioning as someone who in his very body represents the gay scapegoat killed figuratively by conservative elements of the Christian church (and indirectly and literally in the form of suicides and homophobia-inspired hate crimes such as Matthew Shepard's murder). This rhetorical exchange takes place in an online space where, outside of a photo of Lee and in some cases small photos or avatars of the numerous commenters, no one is physically represented or present. Often such rhetorical conditions become environments in which people feel comfortable being a far worse version of themselves than they may be in person. However, the disembodied nature of this exchange may actually have facilitated its civil nature in that the words and language become the focus rather than Lee's (gay) body.

Lee also avoids using the ultimate insulting words to evangelical Christians where homosexuality is concerned—*bigots* and *haters*—the topic that formed one of the questions in the "Ask a Gay Christian" exchange, which I quote here in its entirety.

> FROM KARL: Is it possible in your view for someone to disagree with you—to believe that the Bible consistently teaches sexual activity is intended for heterosexual marriage only—and for that person to not be a bigot, homophobe, motivated by ignorance or fear?

> JUSTIN: Absolutely! Some of my best friends disagree with me on this issue. I recognize that we are all fallible human beings, which means that either (or both) of us could be wrong, but that doesn't mean we aren't sincerely trying to seek the truth. There are bigots who use religious language to justify their hatred, but that doesn't mean that anyone who has a view I disagree with is a bigot. There are also many compassionate, loving Christians who sincerely want to be able to give their blessing to their gay friends' relationships but are unable to because they believe the Bible forbids those relationships. I absolutely respect that.
>
> The same is true on the other side. . . . I am sincerely seeking to do God's will with all my heart. If I am wrong, I am sincerely wrong. I'm not just looking for excuses. All of us, on both sides, need to be willing to assume good motives for those we disagree with. We don't have to agree with each other to make a genuine attempt to understand each other.[22]

By assuming good motives of his audience and those who disagree with him, Lee opens up a rare discursive space among LGBTQ people and evangelical Christians. By conceding that conservative Christians who disagree with him may have good motives behind their stance against homosexuality, he implicitly makes the point that he should be given the same respect and treatment in return. When I asked about his strategy in the exchange above with Karl, Lee described his approach of choosing to focus on motives behind the words of those he disagrees with in an attempt to build goodwill and foster listening.

> A big part of my strategy is putting myself in the other person's shoes. If I'm going to do that, I need to respond to them in a way that's consistent with their (usually good) intentions rather than demonizing them based on the negative results of their actions. . . . I look for the best in people, assume their motives are good, and respect their views even when they differ from mine, focusing on what is most important and agreeing to disagree on the rest. My motto is that everyone is the protagonist of their own story, and I try to treat them accordingly.
>
> Overall, the results I've seen are tremendous. People often tell me—as with the Rachel Held Evans post—that I've said things they've never heard before, even though the things I'm saying have been said many other times by many other people. So even though I'm far from the first to say these things, I've said them in a way that enabled the other person to truly *hear* what was being said, and that's always encouraging.[23]

Whether or not his audience's intentions are good or not is really beside the point: in this exchange his approach overcame extreme rhetorical impasses between two groups normally at odds with one another and caused readers who were resistant to gay rights to listen to him and consider ways of thinking antithetical to conservative Christian discourse.

MUTUAL EXCHANGE AND SELF-CRITIQUE: RHETORICAL EXCHANGE AS AN ONGOING PROCESS

Lee's rhetoric functions in the vein of feminist approaches to rhetoric in that he positions himself as part of a larger, ongoing conversation about how two polarized groups can come together and change one another rather than (only) focusing on how he can change his audience. He makes himself vulnerable and writes from a stance of humility to help disarm antigay rhetoric and the resistance of his audience to listen to a gay man challenge their beliefs. In our interview, he described his approach of using stories to make himself vulnerable rather than challenging his audience directly.

> Rhetorically speaking, someone who bares their soul and talks about the difficult, shameful, or challenging parts of their life is far more compelling than the activist who assumes a posture of confidence and strength and tries to tell you why you're wrong about everything you believe. So my approach is to be vulnerable and let people get to know me for who I am, not who they might have imagined me to be. Once we see each other as fellow human beings and not as stand-ins for sides in a culture war, we can begin the conversation about how we disagree and why.[24]

Lee also stresses that engagement with a topic as difficult as the intersection of sexuality/gender and religion is a process, not a static belief that occurs overnight or changes suddenly. He writes that he "wrestled for a very long time" with the question of what to do with the six passages in the Bible that deal with same-sex issues and with how he'd been taught to view homosexuality within his church and cultural context. At the end of the "Ask a Gay Christian" exchange, he invites his audience to "stay in conversation even though we don't all agree." His emphasis centers on the process of learning and understanding, grounded in stories, rather than on necessarily bringing people to the point where he is in his own activism, as he described in the interview:

> I don't think it's realistic for me to instantly change [my audience's] minds on every point where we might disagree, even if I might like to. So I focus on whatever I think is most pressing. In many cases, I find that the biggest issue is a . . . basic lack of understanding of LGBTQ people's lives that underlies a lot of the conflict we see on these issues. My goal, then, is to increase that understanding. Some LGBTQ advocates want to go in with rhetorical guns blazing and require people to be ready to

accept the whole package of things they believe in—civil marriage equality, church marriage equality, a different reading of
the Bible, abandonment of the gender binary, and whatever
else—when these folks are still trying to wrap their minds around
the idea that some people are attracted to the same sex.

I know that some of those advocates would see some elements
of my language and approach as an unacceptable compromise,
but to me, it's just the simple acknowledgement that people have
to learn to crawl before they can walk. If I can convince someone
not to kick their son out of the house or stop pushing him into
ex-gay therapy, I've accomplished something, even if this person
still goes to the polls and votes against marriage equality.[25]

He argues in his posts that personal experience and investment will be what causes a shift in understanding on this issue,
not logical arguments, and he makes clear that shifts in understanding occur over time and are a process. Such a long view
of rhetorical engagement—attempting mutual understanding
rather than immediate persuasion or change—forms another
important aspect of rhetorical empathy. His example situates
rhetorical empathy as a process based on reflection and mutual
exchange rather than a monologue intended to persuade a
monolithic, stereotyped audience. Such an approach complicates the us-and-them binary that has constructed much of
gay-rights/religious discourse and leaves the door open for further discussion.

ADDRESSING DIFFERENCE, POWER, AND
EMBODIMENT: APPEALS FOR JUSTICE

Rhetorical empathy facilitates connections and understanding
between interlocutors. Such connections create openings that
allow Lee—from the position of someone with less power in
terms of his sexual identity—to highlight power differentials
and injustice, pointing out ways his audience has been complicit
in or overtly responsible for the suffering of LGBTQ people in
their families and faith communities.

Straight guys, do you remember what it was like to be 16 years old
with raging hormones, completely unable to get your mind off of

girls no matter what you did? Well, that was my life too, except it was my male classmates who made my hormones go wild, not my female classmates. . . . When a young man is gay, the message he gets isn't to wait until the right time; it's that there will never be a right time. Not only that; he's told that his sex drive itself—not even lust but just the temptation he feels—is a horrible sin, something that may condemn him to hell even if he never acts on it. Kids who hear these messages feel trapped. They've been made to feel that they're condemned even if they follow all the rules, and many grow to hate themselves.[26]

Lee appeals to the values of his audience: religious devotion and adherence to (their understanding of) orthodox Biblical teaching on sexuality. How can they expect him to follow the teachings of Christianity where sexuality is concerned ("Wait until marriage") if there will never *be* a right time for him and others like him. Using himself as an example, he creates an analogy for his straight male readers, asking them indirectly what they would do in his situation. By using his story and being vulnerable with his readers, he creates an opening to be more direct with them in challenging the basic unfairness and lack of compassion in conservative Christian interpretations of scripture on the topic of homosexuality. His own subject position as a male, it must be said, helps him a great deal in his efforts to appeal to his audience. As a male, even a gay-identified male, Lee does not encounter the same resistance as women who speak against homophobia, sexism, and racism among evangelical Christians.

RHETORICAL EMPATHY'S VALUE FOR NAVIGATING DIFFERENCE

Positioning an audience as part of a spectrum rather than monolith, as individuals with contexts and motivations important to their position and as people who are in the process of becoming, offers potential for rhetorical engagement that goes beyond Crowley's notion of civil discourse. Lee's example demonstrates that possibilities exist for engaging with people Crowley would characterize as fundamentalists but who are willing to listen and consider other viewpoints. Rhetorical empathy entails treating such individuals as real people with stories and motivations of their own rather than responding with patronization and anger or relying on logical arguments to refute stereotypes and ignorance.

The responses to Lee's rhetorical strategies in the "Ask a Gay Christian" exchange are positive. One comment by a reader points to the efficacy of rhetorical empathy in Lee's example:

> You, Justin, are perhaps one of the most mature people I've ever met. Wow. I'm blown away, really. I've never read anything from either side of this issue that is as mature, reflective, or nuanced as yours. You, sir, are the kind of person that needs to be doing the talking on the TV networks and magazine stories. I, like many others here I'm sure, am still undecided . . . as I keep thinking I get all the arguments, but then meeting or hearing from someone (such as yourself) who blows everything up. You've given me a lot to think about, and I wish I could meet you in person. Oh, and Rachel . . . you are to be commended, as I know of no others (in my "camp" or not, so to speak) who would do something like this. Very insightful and cool.[27]

This reader's comments highlight the fact that Lee's rhetorical strategies in this online forum opened up spaces that seem impossible or at least are rare.

It's impossible to know exactly what the motivations were of those who engaged Lee in this question-and-answer forum. Based on the fact they self-selected to participate and use their names in a public, online forum suggests they were fairly open about their desire to learn more about those on the other side of gay-rights battles on the religious right. Even if we assume his interlocutors do not represent evangelical Christians who ardently believe being gay is wrong and must be legislated against or at the least ignored in a don't-ask-don't-tell fashion, the fact that he was able to engage in productive dialogue with self-described evangelicals on this issue is significant.

Considering the motivations of others—seeing them as individuals and as part of larger discourses that shape them—in an attempt to genuinely understand them as fellow humans with hurts and fears of their own does not automatically equal acquiescence, naivety, or a lack of power. Lee's use of rhetorical empathy suggests that such a stance can become a source of agency for people in nondominant positions precisely because of the connections rhetors make with an Other through narrative and emotional appeals. Such connections allow them to highlight the body, difference, and injustice in the process.

4

BEYOND "COMMON GROUND"
Rhetorical Empathy in Composition Pedagogies

*For over 20 years, I have understood, taught, and practiced
academic writing as being at its base about argument, and
I regard it as a very political thing. But I am SO ready to
be post-argument. Or maybe it's just post-Aristotelian and
post-Toulminian. In writing this, I have thought about what
other theories and models of argumentation might drive
FYC. Why so little, for example, on Rogerian argument? And
I wonder how Wendy Bishop might invite me to think about
argument, curriculum, and FYC.*
—Post on the Writing Program
Administrators listserv

All knowledge ultimately is personal.
—Michael Polanyi

I'll never forget an experience I had in a first-semester writing
class at Baruch College at the City University of New York in the
fall of 2015. I had themed the course around race, and I told my
class of around fifteen students—a night class with the kind of
diverse students for which CUNY is famous—that I was taking
the class along with them. The previous summer Eric Garner
had been killed nearby in Staten Island by police officers for
the crime of selling loose cigarettes, and the Black Lives Matter movement had formed in response to the death of Michael
Brown and so many other black women and men killed by law
enforcement across the country.

As my students were trying to decide how to narrow their
research questions for their major project, one student, a
white male from Staten Island, made the case in his written
proposal that the Black Lives Matter movement was making

DOI: 10.7330/9781607329107.c004

cops' lives more difficult. The sources he included all were from Breitbart.com. I asked him who the audience was for his paper: who was he imagining as he wrote? He couldn't answer, even though I'd asked the class to use that heuristic to think with as they approached their project. I asked him to consider imagining a black male who had experienced police violence and was an activist with Black Lives Matter as his audience and to choose sources that might be persuasive to him, since Breitbart News likely would not. I asked him to consider how he had come to believe his thesis as well, but in the end, he couldn't write the paper as he'd imagined it. Not, I believe, because he thought I would be unfair in grading him but because the exercise of imagining that particular audience and writing about his experiences likely was too much of a stretch for him to make. Maybe his father or uncle or mother was a police office in Staten Island. I'll never know. I do know that asking students (and ourselves) to interrogate through story the *how* and *why* we've come to believe the way we do is a powerful way to learn and enlarge our perspectives.

The kind of empathy and change that can occur as a result of what Michael Polanyi calls "personal knowledge"—the basis of rhetorical empathy—represents a valuable means of persuasion, one that has been downplayed in composition courses focused on argumentation as a primary genre in recent years. The kind of deep listening and knowledge that can result from using personal stories as a way of knowing and engaging with others resists the tired, mostly useless trope of finding common ground we hear so often in discussions about civic discourse. Rhetorical empathy has bearing on the teaching of writing and rhetoric in US higher education within two primary threads in the field of writing studies: the first is the role of "personal writing" in composition (versus analytical or argumentative) and the second is the way argumentative or persuasive writing typically is taught using an Aristotelian and Toulmin-based model. In this chapter, I trace both these threads briefly in recent scholarship in the field and share examples of how elements of rhetorical empathy have played out in my classes.

Personal writing in composition classes has materialized over the past few decades in the form of the narrative mode, its current iteration the literacy narrative. The argument-focused expository mode has, since the 1990s, gained dominance in first-year writing. A long, storied history exists in writing studies over the place of the personal in composition, most notably the Elbow-Bartholomae debate and before that in the work of Ann Berthoff and the lesser-known work of theorist Walter Fisher on the narrative paradigm. In recent years, prominent voices such as Wendy Bishop and Doug Hesse have advocated for the place of creative writing in composition. Eli Goldblatt in his *College Composition and Communication* piece on personal writing, "Don't Call It Expressivism: Legacies of a 'Tacit' Tradition," reconsiders the role of the personal in composition theory and practice. He argues that students are more persuaded by the efficacy of personal stories than by logical arguments or even other kinds of emotional appeals. While acknowledging the significant contribution of movements with the field such as writing about writing and transfer studies, he worries that moves toward student success and professionalization "have oriented the discussion about writing instruction too narrowly."[1] Rather than pick and choose between two sides of a coin, he suggests we see expressivism as "not gone but woven into our present ways of understanding writers" and that recovering its place in the field "will add to our core strength as a discipline faced with daunting social, administrative, and intellectual challenges in the American and global literacy scene."[2]

His advocacy of personal writing resonates with Anne Ellen Geller, Michele Eodice, and Neal Lerner's *The Meaningful Writing Project*, a national study of how seniors perceived the writing they've done in college. The study suggests that the assignments that stayed with students were those they found personally meaningful and relevant to their lives. Goldblatt values personal writing for personal expression and for connecting with communities in need, and I argue that we should combine these more deliberately and often in light of the challenges we face, not only within the academy but as citizens. The power of story in argument is hard to deny given the rhetorical power of the students from Marjory Stoneman Douglas High School in Parkland, Florida, and across the United States who have experienced gun violence firsthand and have spoken out for change on legislative and societal levels.

THE FUNCTION OF "PERSUASIVE" WRITING IN COMPOSITION

The division Aristotle makes between rhetoric and poetics began a binary relationship between narrative and rhetoric that still exists. This binary, and the taxonomies that are so important to Aristotelian philosophy, has been tremendously influential in how we think about discourse and how we teach composition. In the second-most influential text on rhetorical theory in the Euro-American tradition after Aristotle's *Rhetoric*, George Campbell in *The Philosophy of Rhetoric* creates a taxonomy of the purposes of rhetoric, dividing it into four categories: "All the ends of speaking are reducible to four; every speech being intended to enlighten the understanding, to please the imagination, to move the passions, or to influence the will."[3] These categories roughly have translated into the discrete modes of exposition, narrative, and argument in composition textbooks and pedagogy since the late nineteenth century, where they continue, mostly uncontested, today. Even though Aristotle blurs the lines between these categories, his taxonomy still functions as a commonplace, deeply embedded in the operating assumptions of those who study and teach college English courses, so it's often difficult to imagine the generative cross-disciplinary benefits of deconstructing the narrative/argument binary.

Another consequence of holding to Campbell's taxonomy and privileging Aristotle as the foundational rhetorical text for rhetoric and composition as a discipline is that the teaching of nonfiction writing in composition courses and beyond has privileged rhetoric-as-persuasion. Not only has rhetoric and composition privileged persuasion and argument, it has privileged argument of a certain kind, and with profound consequences.[4]

In her article "A Textbook Argument: Definitions of Argument in Leading Composition Textbooks," A. Abby Knoblauch explores the prominence of rhetoric-as-argument in the most widely circulated, influential composition textbooks of the past decade, suggesting that even though rhetorics such as Andrea Lunsford and John J. Ruszkiewicz's *Everything's an Argument* and John D. Ramage, John C. Bean, and June Johnson's *Writing Arguments* position all discourse as rhetorical in nature, the purpose each textbook proposes for rhetoric is to persuade an audience (and, in keeping with Aristotelian theory, to discover the ways discourse is persuading us).

Rhetoric-as-argument as a vestige of Aristotelian epistemology centers on changing an Other rather than listening and seeing the world through an Other's eyes. The results of this focus are countless textbooks and papers in English classes and beyond that privilege the presence of a thesis or argument and its clear defense, usually with logos-based evidence void of the personal in the form of narrative and experience. The personal in the form of stories and emotion is devalued at best and actively denigrated at worst. As a response, this project represents a re-viewing of pathos—the personal, the emotional, and their political implications—unmooring it from its Aristotelian roots and tracing its function within influential Enlightenment, modern, and postmodern rhetorical theory and making a case for rhetorical empathy as a topos for effective rhetorical engagement and as a way of changing ourselves.

In the same vein, Dennis A. Lynch, Diana George, and Marilyn Cooper position persuasion in the context of rhetorical education as about change not only within an audience but within a rhetor, holding that "we need to see [argumentation] not just as a matter of winning or losing but as a way to connect with others which may lead to change, not only in the world but also in ourselves."[5] In "Moments of Argument: Agonistic Inquiry and Confrontational Cooperation," they advocate creating pedagogical spaces where conflict and affirmation are both possible. They acknowledge the value of Susan Jarratt's "case for conflict," in which she argues against the idea of a nurturing environment in composition classes.[6] She advocates a pedagogical approach in which the body and difference are highlighted and in which "conflict is central," writing that "differences of gender, race, and class among students and teachers provide situations in which conflict does arise, and we need more than the ideal of the harmonious, nurturing composition class in our repertory of teaching practices to deal with these problems."[7] Lynch, George, and Cooper, however, resist the either/or binary of conflict or collaboration, holding that "serious argumentation requires a willingness to see things differently and to be changed in and through the dialogic process."[8]

As with Lindquist's strategic empathy, and as with moves associated with Rogerian rhetoric,[9] the process Lynch, George, and Cooper describe associates a reduction of threat with the likelihood of change. They point out that in their experience, students tend to be more open to risk changing after they feel some sort of connection or a safe environment to help motivate them to listen: "We believe that students will risk such changes only when argumentation is perceived as a social activity through which they, first and foremost, connect with others."[10] However, they point out that change most often is accompanied by the pain that can be involved when we open ourselves to an Other's perspective, and that in fact we often experience change for the better precisely through struggle and conflict and because we've made the decision to truly hear another perspective.

Another implication of rhetorical empathy for pedagogy—and the focus of this chapter—is the use of personal experience and stories as a valuable kind of epistemology and evidence within research-based contexts in academic writing. Rhetorical strategies characterized by a strategic kind of empathy are in keeping with the feminist political philosophy that the personal is always political. Empathy is grounded in pathos and the personal, but it has potential for political power as well. In *The Activist WPA: Changing Stories about Writing and Writers*, Adler-Kassner points out that "stories serve as connections between individual experience and broader cultures and communities."[11] The use of the personal in the form of stories disarms an audience through identification ("You're like me on some level") and so can help bridge gaps in understanding across marked social differences. It is an extension of Toulmin's qualifier on an emotional, personal level, which ideally should not be used to manipulate an audience or to (only) try to get one's point across but to open avenues of understanding—in many ways the very essence of learning (that is, changing). The tropes and speech acts that result from pedagogies based on rhetorical empathy include stories that resist stereotypes, and narratives that are based on the personal as a way of knowing.[12] Such narratives result from seeing the Other as an individual who is part of a larger system, but an individual nonetheless, and such rhetorical moves invite an audience to adopt the same topos and tropes in turn. Rhetorical empathy invokes change as (and because) it disarms.

NARRATIVE ARGUMENT: COMBINING
THE PERSONAL AND POLITICAL

An example of rhetorical empathy that combines personal writing in the form of stories and public-directed writing in the classroom is an assignment I developed in my first-year writing courses at Baruch College. It combines elements of a literacy narrative and public-argument project, building on students' experiences and stories and connecting them to larger issues that affect their lives. We have two required courses: an academic writing-focused course scaffolding into a second-semester course that involves an extended research project with a public-directed, multimodal writing component. A large number of creative writers teach in our program, and as writing director I've encouraged incorporating a literacy narrative or creative nonfiction as a way of entering into the thematic focus for the course using a personal epistemological lens. We also include a significant research project as part of our curriculum, but until this particular assignment, I hadn't before blended the two kinds of writing as deliberately, and as fruitfully, as I describe here.

I asked students at the beginning of the term to write a literacy narrative about their experience with language and with

English in particular, and about the cultural capitol literacy entails, both for them and their family. Later in the term, for a public-argument assignment, I asked them to advocate change on some level (in thinking or action) in literacy education or public access to education. Most important for my purposes here, I asked them to consciously bring in elements of the short literacy narrative they'd written earlier, emphasizing that not only is it okay to use their story as a way to move and inform their audience but that it actually could be the most powerful form of evidence for their advocacy claim. Since this assignment was their major research project for the term, I asked them to conduct research using databases and to write reflective annotated bibliographies and incorporate at least four sources along with their own stories. We discussed the problematic and challenging nature of using the personal in academic writing, framing the subject as one based on power, personal ethos, and intersectional subject positions, as well as the norms established by discourse communities.

Following is the assignment I have since called Narrative Argument, drawing on Excelsior College's Online Writing Lab's name for assignments blending storytelling and persuasion:[13]

> Earlier in the term I asked you to write a narrative about your and your family's experience with English, education, and literacy. In particular I asked you to write in response to the following questions: What role has education played in your family's life? How has your family's background influenced your own decision to come to college (or not)? What role has your family's ethnic or racial background and/or social class played in your education and relationship to literacy (reading and writing)? For this Narrative Argument project, I want you to revisit that narrative you wrote and think about how it connects to larger, public issues around literacy, education, and race or ethnicity. Your own story can—and should—serve as a powerful form of evidence and an example supporting your larger argument. I will ask that you not only draw from your own experiences and memories to write this paper; you should cite at least four sources in your paper besides your own and/or your family's story. You should establish an audience for your project, and your sources of evidence should be credible and persuasive to them.

This assignment offers a number of insights about the value of using personal stories within argument genres in which students research a topic and make an argument based on one or more topoi such as fact, definition, quality, cause, or policy. The first is that student writing is far more interesting to read, at least for me, and students told me in their reflections on this assignment that using their stories provided not only a starting point for their research but also made their writing more interesting to them. Many students started their pieces with their own stories, creating a compelling hook often missing from academic writing and research projects in particular. One student, Autumn Madden, drew the conclusion from her own story and her research that more resources are needed in high school for first-generation students preparing for college. Like many students in the class, she incorporated large passages from her literacy narrative about being a first-generation student into her position paper. Here she describes the experience of using her own story not only as evidence, but as the impetus behind her interest in her topic:

> To write this draft I gathered credible information from multiple sources and sifted through them to decide which ones to do my Reflective Annotative Bibliography on. I focused on what I knew first, my story, and the story of my parents. Speaking from experience develops powerful, descriptive language, and incredible detail. The power of a personal anecdote is unmatched. From here I branched out to speak about larger issues affecting America as a whole, based on my own experiences. I also looked at the other side of the perspective to further strengthen my argument by countering their points.

Another student, Kamran Malik, used his story from the earlier writing he'd done in the term almost verbatim in his position paper, tailoring it a bit for a different context. His original literacy narrative reads,

> In my opinion, education is one of the most important things an individual can invest into because not only does it help them find a job but it makes them a well-rounded individual who is open-minded to different cultures around the world. I think my parents have played and are playing an important role in my

education. Both of my parents were born into poverty in their native Pakistan. My father was struck with polio as an infant. He was robbed of a life with movement in his right leg. My mother's father passed away when she was a little girl. My mother had to drop out of school to help support the family, rather unconventional in patriarchal Pakistan. She worked in crop fields and herded sheep, giving all of her earnings to her mother. Realizing the difficulties of providing for a child in Pakistan, my parents decided to leave for a better life in America, something that many Pakistanis desire, yet are not able to do. Despite my father's health condition and our family's socio-economic status, my parents somehow managed to get to the United States. My father has worked practically every day since he arrived in the United States, providing not only for us at home, but his family in Pakistan as well. In spite of his polio, my father is a cab driver. He uses his left leg to shift between the pedals. It is a tough life for him, I have no doubt. I see it in his eyes when he comes home from work and I happen to be up studying late at night. I want to live a respectable life earning a decent salary so that my parents can enjoy the rest of their lives without being concerned about having enough food on the table, good quality health care, or living in a better community. The way I see it, my parents have taken me this far, now it is my turn to catapult us into a lifestyle that provides us with comfort and a quality standard of living.

From his Narrative Argument paper, "From Pakistan to America: Language Struggles of an Immigrant Family":

My knowledge of my families history only extends as far back as my parents because of language and geographical barriers that have severed relationships with my family back "home." Both of my parents were born into poverty in their native country, Pakistan. From a young age, both of my parents struggled, but both of them only struggled from their socio-economic position. My father was struck with polio as an infant, and due to the fact that his family could not afford medical services, he was robbed of a life with movement in his right leg. Because he was disabled to an extent, he lived his life in Pakistan struggling to find employment so that he can meet his most basic needs. My mother's life was also plagued with hardship. Her father passed away when she was a little girl leaving her with only her mother in a place and time where it was difficult to support oneself, let alone a family as a single mother. My mother had to drop out of school to help support the family, a rather unconventional move in what was then and continues to be a patriarchal Pakistan where women remain at home. She worked in crop fields and herded sheep, giving all of her earnings to her mother until she married my father. Although both were disadvantaged in their own ways, my mother disadvantaged by her position as a woman, and my father disadvantaged by his disability, they were both disadvantaged by the never ending cycle of poverty that trapped many people in rural areas in Pakistan and bordering South-Asian countries. While we only faced socio-economic hardship in Pakistan, in the United States my family, like many immigrant families, we were met with intersectional struggles that compounded against each other. My family's struggles were all spurred by language which affected them in other ways such as discrimination, social class, and internalized shame as a result of being LEP (Limited English Proficient), which I will also refer to as linguistic terrorism (a term coined by Gloria Anzaldua).

Kamran's story is especially powerful, touching on his motivations for going to college and learning English and also pushing back on the ways multilingualism is undervalued in the United States. Interestingly, he provides poignant details, especially about his father, in his original literacy narrative that he omits in his position paper, maybe as a result of his hesitations over blending too much personal writing and details into an academic argument. Like other students, he expressed in his reflections the difficulty of knitting together the threads of personal and so-called academic writing, indicating that students are conditioned to treat academic writing as depersonalized and removed from the stories of their lives. He alludes to this possibility somewhat in his reflection on the assignment, mentioning the difficulty in blending two modes of writing that usually are kept distinct.

> The title of my paper is "From Pakistan to America: Language Struggles of an Immigrant Family." The audience I have in mind for my piece is students who I want to understand how language poses a barrier in so many different aspects in the lives of immigrants. This makes a difference in how I'm approaching my paper because I am showing my audience how this has affected my life and the life of my family. The purpose for my piece is to show how lack of language access is a social injustice and how language can be oppressive. My thesis is Lack of language access

programs and initiatives in regards to education, employment, and healthcare leads many immigrants to becoming victims of medical malpractice or negligence, watered down education curriculum and a disconnect between parents and their children's education, and difficulty finding employment which contributes to high poverty rates among immigrants. I support it in the following ways: (a) by using only scholarly peer reviewed sources which are reliable and (b) incorporating quotes from the sources in order to get my point across. The hardest part of this project has been incorporating the sources and the reflective annotated bibliography because I have little to no experience with both. What I think I've done well is organize my paper and incorporate my thesis throughout as Dr. Blankenship suggested when I received feedback. What I think needs more work is the incorporation of my sources into the paper. I feel like they make the paper choppy. My questions for you as readers are

1. Was my paper convincing in helping you understand language access issues?

2. Do you feel my sources validated my points?

3. How do you feel the narratives and the sources worked together? Did they complement each other well?

Kamran identifies his thesis as relating to the disadvantages immigrants to the United States experience because of a lack of access to ELL programs and also the shame resulting from being in a culture that still mostly values monolingualism. He first mentions his use of his back story as a way of connecting with his audience of his peers, who he points out may not realize the degree of the struggles immigrant families face. Many students chose to address their arguments to an audience who also has a personal connection and vested interest in their subject. For example, many chose an audience like themselves: other 1.5-generation immigrants attempting to balance their home and school communities, or other first-generation immigrants who are parents. This audience focus gave them a sense of authority to speak and more of a buy-in to the research they conducted. Kamran struggles, though, to make a connection between his story and the authoritative outside sources he cites in his paper. When I asked what kind of evidence he'd used to support his thesis, he pointed to "scholarly peer reviewed sources in order to get my point across." Like Kamran, other students in their reflections also did not make the explicit connection that their story was a kind of evidence even though they used it as such, pointing again to the degree to which depersonalized writing is a commonplace in academic settings.

This assignment functions as a form of rhetorical empathy in the following ways: it asks students to use their own stories as a way of learning about what they already know and as a way of forming new knowledge as they pursue a research project on a topic they care about—one related to their own experience in some way. It goes beyond giving students "license" to use personal anecdotes as a form of evidence to persuade an audience; rather it considers the personal a valid way of forming knowledge, especially when stories based on personal experience are held against or alongside other kinds of evidence. Listening to other students' stories becomes a way of understanding the "back story" behind a thesis or argument and can help make an audience seem real rather than a stereotype. This assignment functions like Lee's rhetorical move of inviting his audience to consider the stories behind how he changed his mind about gay people. This rhetorical decision helps disarm his audience so the issue at hand—greater understanding and acceptance of queer people in conservative Christian families and churches—becomes framed by personal stories and appeals to love rather than theological arguments.

In some ways, empathy can be boiled down to a focus on audience and trying to best anticipate what communicative approach will be most effective. In my own teaching, principles of rhetorical empathy remind me to try imagining what it's like to be a student in my class. One of the most important contributions rhetorical empathy adds to composition theory and pedagogy is an emphasis on students as real people with stories and motivations behind their responses in class. This focus on students affects every aspect of pedagogy, from how we write syllabi and assignments and design our curriculum to how we try to anticipate how students may react to a particular reading and discussion about it. I think about the idea of rhetorical empathy also in relation to teaching multimodal assignments and new technologies. I try to remember what it was like for me the first time I opened a new software application and felt overwhelmed at the possibilities and frustrated because I didn't even know how to begin. It's easy for us to forget what it is like to be in the position of our students and important to try to remember, even if our experiences will never be exactly the same as theirs.

Relatedly, another implication of rhetorical empathy for pedagogy is the importance of doing work along with our students whenever possible. Just as we help students with the invention process because we (hopefully) try to think about how frustrating it is to stare at a blank screen and not have a clue where to begin, it's important for writing teachers to be writers and equally important for those of us who incorporate multimodal assignments to use various modes in our own work and to practice (and fail) along with students. In 1975, Jim Corder wrote in "What I Learned at School" about his experience of actually writing the papers he asked his students to complete. Engaging with the assignments gave him greater perspective on his role as a writing teacher that he hadn't been able to see from his role as a scholarly writer in his own research. In a similar vein, E. Shelley Reid writes about the importance of asking graduate students in TA training courses to compose assignments they'll ask students to write. Reid argues that "writing pedagogy classes need to provide writing experiences that allow students to experience productive, guided difficulty in writing—and thus to become true learners in the field. Working through these difficulties within a supportive environment will increase teachers' empathy with students."[14] In graduate courses, most students (some of whom go on to become faculty) don't get the kind of hands-on, reflective, workshop-model experience of peer editing and revising work we ask of students in our composition classes, whether in alphabetic-text assignments or those engaging with multiple modes of composing.

On a few occasions, I've been able to do my assignments along with my students. The first time was several years ago in a digital writing and rhetoric class I taught as a doctoral student at Miami University. The other was in a digital storytelling course I developed at Baruch College recently. In both cases, the experience caused me to relate to my students differently, to better anticipate their questions, and to grade differently. I gained new kinds of technological literacy working with recording equipment and software, but maybe more important, I gained experiential literacy after feeling the frustration and excitement of recording myself reading a story I'd written for the project and then listening to my literal and figurative voice embodied in a digital artifact, as was the case when I created a podcast along with my students—a first for me. I experienced the frustration and satisfaction of remixing multiple layers of sound, such as music and voice tracks, to compose in an entirely new genre. I realized in several cases that their work was far more advanced than what I was doing. Part of my issue, as it is with all of us, was a lack of time to put into the assignment, but even this aspect comes to bear on the amount of work I assign and the expectations I have of students who are juggling courses, work, and extracurricular responsibilities.

It was good for me to feel—and I stress the word *feel*—what it's like to open a new program and not have a clue what it does or how to make it do what I want it to do. It's one thing for me to teach a writing assignment or a software application I've used for years and an entirely different experience to teach something new. The latter puts us in a position to learn along with students, and just as with making ourselves vulnerable by listening to students and trying to understand what motivates them, it requires risk on our part as instructors. Learning along with students is a kind of surface acting, to use Lindquist's theory, but decentering the classroom and admitting we don't always know the best way to proceed can become forms of deep acting and normalized aspects of our pedagogy.

Another way principles of rhetorical empathy can play out in the classroom is through the use of writing groups, which I've used in my classes for many years, carefully selecting groups of (usually) three to work together all semester to discuss readings and their writing at various stages. I explain that the writing groups I've been in have made possible almost every piece of writing I've done, normalizing the process of talking through ideas and getting feedback on a work in progress. I usually try to bring in various heavily edited drafts of a piece of writing I've published to show them that feedback and revision are not only to be expected but can improve your writing and thinking.

Qualley in *Turns of Thought* discusses the use of writing groups not only for feedback on written drafts but also for the purpose of getting other perspectives on whatever topics students are working through. This practice brings the idea of public writing into the classroom, breaking down the binaries of classroom/public and personal/academic writing. Her use of writing groups for this purpose supports what she calls *reflexive practice*: "getting at the *why* behind our beliefs, interrogating our beliefs as we compare them to others' and to our past selves."[15] For her, reflection is what an individual does within themself, a unidirectional thought process; reflexive practice, she writes, "occurs in response to a person's critical engagement with an 'other.'"[16] A key term for her, one that emerges in Krista Ratcliffe's *Rhetorical Listening* and this work as well, is *understanding*: "In the process of trying to understand an other, our own beliefs and assumptions are disclosed, and these assumptions, themselves, can become objects of examination and critique."[17] Reflexive practice occurs in an in-between space of liminality, a threshold, a place of uncertainty and teachability—a place of learning. For Qualley, the process of writing itself, when it's done in the context of a writing group deeply immersed in reflexive practice, offers the possibility of what she calls "earned insights" similar to those learned through personal experience.[18]

Composition pedagogies based on rhetorical empathy ask students to recognize the contextual and personally situated nature of all arguments and discourse. Unlike Rogerian rhetoric, rhetorical empathy does not ask writers to remove themselves in the form of their experiences or emotions from learning but rather to put their experiences in the context of larger arguments.[19] Rather than summarizing the Other in an

objective way as Rogerian rhetoric asks—an approach criticized on feminist grounds for silencing women and privileging so-called objectivity[20]—rhetorical empathy asks writers to
bring themselves to the subject in the form of personal stories
and to understand the ways their own view of a subject or a
group of people has been shaped by larger cultural discourses.
Rhetorical empathy does not ask that we silence our own perspective but rather that we foreground our emotions and
responses to Others' stories and ask how power is circulating
and functioning in every speech act and rhetorical situation.
How many times have we asked students to write about a topic
only to realize all their sources have come from news outlets
that reinforce their views? Rhetorical empathy resists the echo
chamber of contemporary, digital, and political culture and
forces us to engage with the Other in the form of real people
with real stories that, chances are, do not align with our own
understanding of the world.

Epilogue
A THEORY OF RHETORICAL EMPATHY

I stood at the rail looking down at the ocean and saw the foil-like flickering of flying fish, and it struck me that knowledge is always open to change. . . . If it is not open to change it is not knowledge, it is prejudice.
—Madeline L'Engle, *And It Was Good: Reflections on Beginnings*

I cannot muster the "we" except by finding the way in which I am tied to "you," by trying to translate but finding that my own language must break up and yield if I am to know you. You are what I gain through this disorientation and loss. This is how the human comes into being, again and again, as that which we have yet to know.
—Judith Butler, *Precarious Life: The Powers of Mourning and Violence*

By focusing on rhetors who have successfully employed rhetorical empathy, I demonstrate its possibilities. Rhetorical thinking, writing, and speaking—even the ways we use our bodies in the world—all are part of a process. Each rhetorical engagement we have, each speech act and digital story in the examples I analyze, is connected to previous ones in our own stories, and each one will in some way determine the next ones we have. Rhetoric never is isolated, and rhetorical empathy increases the possibilities for less toxic, more effective ways of connecting across difference in sustained ways. Social media has disconnected us into bubbles and echo chambers, but Joyce Fernandes and Justin Lee are examples of how the circulatory reach of social media can enable not only connection across profound difference but also avenues for activism—never uncomplicated—that would not be available otherwise.

DOI: 10.7330/9781607329107.c005

In suggesting ways rhetorical empathy can help facilitate engagement across difference, my intention is not to oversimplify its usefulness. Rhetorical engagements are part of ongoing discourses, and agency occurs within discourse as kairotic and shifting, with numerous constraints. Among the most significant constraints of rhetorical empathy are power differences, depending on the various ways we identify intersectionally. Female rhetors have faced discrimination within social movements in the United States historically, the most prominent example of which was when women began participating in public campaigns against slavery in the mid-nineteenth century, advocating for women's rights after they faced a great deal of backlash for speaking publicly in the presence of men. Addams faced similar constraints because of her gender. For example, less than a year after she delivered her speech on domestic-labor issues at the World's Columbian Exposition in Chicago, the railroad titan George Pullman refused to meet with the female members of the Chicago Civic Federation during their attempts to mediate between the company and its workers just before the Pullman strike erupted. Since Addams was the only woman playing a pivotal role in the mediation leading up to what became one of the most significant strikes in US history, and one of only two women on the large committee made of up business and civic leaders, his point of discriminating against her because of her gender was clear.[1]

Becoming vulnerable in any form can be highly problematic for those with relatively less power and in marginalized subject positions. Using an intersectional lens is necessary in thinking about who has power in which circumstance, but regardless of who is employing it, an approach such as rhetorical empathy involves giving up power in certain ways: that is, when we decide to listen to someone's stories and attempt to discern what is motivating them, we choose to be vulnerable—a move that can be productive for anyone but that obviously is riskier and more costly for those in nondominant subject positions. As Ratcliffe points out in *Rhetorical Listening*, identity and identification are finely interwoven. Rhetorical engagement often entails the issue of how much of our identity and identifications with certain people and groups we are willing (or able) to give up in order to engage with an Other.

Another constraint of rhetorical empathy is the degree to which it can seem contrived or manipulative. It's important to note that performing empathy may be sincere on a certain level, and it may, at the same time, be strategic—that is, not necessarily coming from a deeply emotional, honest level but purposefully engaged in to get the other side to consider the ideas being expressed. In the example of surface acting and deep acting in Lindquist's piece on classroom applications of empathy, a rhetor may be angry (or feel any number of emotions) but choose not to respond in anger so they can engage an Other with a degree of compassion. The extent to which such a rhetorical move is sincere is impossible to know, even for ourselves at times, but the sheer power of habit would suggest that the more often rhetors employ an inventional stance based on empathy, the greater such a stance becomes a commonplace, a normalized way of engaging with others, regardless of the degree of offense, injustice, or socially marked difference. This is an important point that is difficult to research, quantify, and measure, even through self-disclosure methods, but it is a fair speculation based on the case studies in this project.

A final constraint I should discuss—and maybe the elephant in the room at this juncture in our country's political and civic life—is that a person must be open to listen and therefore to change for rhetorical empathy to "work" beyond changing the subject/writer/rhetor. It's true that rhetorical empathy can soften a rhetor toward someone who is intractable in their beliefs, but ultimately there must be some kind of opening both ways in order for dialogue to occur. For some, such an opening is not likely to occur, either because they are so entrenched within the discourse of their group that they really can't hear or see beyond it (McComiskey's two-dimensional rhetoric) or because they literally cannot afford to be vulnerable. Some have no interest in seeing beyond their current positions and thinking because they benefit from them. As the example of

Lee highlights, conservative Christian discourse often misrep-
resents queer people in order to justify and perpetuate existing power structures. There is an element of the Christian right
with deeply vested interests in maintaining the status quo in
terms of patriarchal power structures in the church and in society, just as there is a deeply entrenched segment of our society
whose views on racial and ethnic difference are difficult if not
impossible to change.

In *American Grace: How Religion Unites and Divides Us*, Robert
Putnam helps put this demographic in perspective. His research
suggests that approximately 10 percent of Americans are what he
calls "true believers." People in this group do not believe other
religions are valid, they actively try to convert others to their
faith, they are politically conservative, and they tend to associate only with likeminded people on a close basis.[2] If Crowley is
right in her conclusion that the only way to have a true dialogue
with someone in this group is to convert to the group, the possibilities for getting beyond fundamentalism in American life (of
all stripes, not just religious) do in fact seem slim. However, as
Putnam points out, this number is low compared to the majority
of those in the United States who express at least a belief—if not
a practice—of accepting those different from them. Rhetorical
empathy may have some bearing on the 90 percent he describes
as being open to learning and difference.

How, though, do we measure the effectiveness of rhetorical
empathy? How can we track its results in concrete terms? In
other words, what happens after—or as a result of—rhetorical
empathy? What happens when it fails? How do we know it has
succeeded? What happens post rhetorical empathy is difficult to
measure. Like writing and education itself, empathy is a process.
It's recursive, and it's far from uncomplicated. The best gauge
for effective rhetorical empathy may be the degree to which
it leaves the door open for future engagement and gradual
shifts rather than immediate change. For example, in Addams's
case—in the speech I highlight and throughout her life—her
stance of mediation and of challenging both sides of an issue
or conflict to consider the stories and the motivations of the

Other often did not produce immediate changes some might associate with effective rhetoric. Like other peacemakers such as Martin Luther King Jr. and Barack Obama, Addams was criticized for being too conciliatory toward her enemies and sometimes of playing both sides of the fence. Rhetorical empathy offers a way of engaging across difference, though, because it creates openings and possibilities where before there may have been only division and impasse. It has the potential of changing those who think with it—reminding us that everyone is vulnerable in some way and everyone has stories, previous chapters in the book of their lives that may help explain their thinking and actions. Rhetorical empathy may not change the other person; it may not change the issue or circumstances at hand, at least not right away. An approach based on rhetorical empathy increases the chances that openings will occur for engagement and learning—no more, no less. Rhetorical empathy rests on the premise that listening precedes empathy, and empathy precedes understanding. Without understanding no progress ultimately can be made. But that is significant, especially in our current moment.

A memorable example of how complicated (and promising) rhetorical engagements based in empathy can be is the story of Megan Phelps-Roper, the granddaughter of the Westboro Church founder, Fred Phelps. Phelps-Roper eventually left the church after several months of engaging on Twitter with David Abitol, founder of the Jewish culture blog Jewlicious. Instead of responding to her tweets with sarcasm or anger, Abitol used an approach based on humor and compassion. They shared stories about their daily lives and kept a conversation going in the form of frequent tweets rather than shutting down in anger or blocking one another. In a TED Talk, she explains, "There was no confusion about our positions, but the line between friend and foe was becoming blurred. We'd started to see each other as human beings, and it changed the way we spoke to one another."[3] Finally, they met up at a protest Westboro Baptist held at an event Abitol helped arrange, and they exchanged gifts rather than yelling at one another. Her defenses began to crack, and his approach toward her led her to start questioning the hateful tactics she'd been immersed in her entire life.

Among many other things, her story speaks to McComiskey's argument about the rise of digital media facilitating three-dimensional rhetorics, as polarizing as social media can be. It also points to the potential of social media to create connections that never would be possible or would be unlikely otherwise. All too frequently, the anonymity of the internet can foster trolls and online harassment, especially against women. As the examples of Lee, Fernandes, and Phelps-Roger suggest, however, social media also allows interlocutors to interact with people they may never encounter in their lives outside the internet. It also allows them to read people's stories and reflect on them without the instantaneous pressure of a face-to-face encounter.[4]

A response based on anger or on believing the worst about someone can close doors for future engagement. Sometimes, for various reasons we could fill a book with, closing doors and drawing boundaries are necessary for self-preservation. Rhetorical empathy isn't always the best choice. It's one strategy among many other forms of rhetorical engagement. In certain situations, anger or rhetorical refusal are better responses.[5] For example, gay-rights activists frequently use in-group, performative expressions such as *drag* and *camp* as a form of resistance. In the 1980s and 90s, groups such as ACT UP and the Sisters of Perpetual Indulgence (gay men who donned nun habits in protest of the Catholic church's stance on "homosexuality" during the AIDS crisis) used disruption as a rhetorical strategy. It's hard to imagine protest movements such as Black Lives Matter and #MeToo exposing sexual harassment and assault operating under the principles of rhetorical empathy. Sometimes anger, protest, and shock are exactly what are required to bring long overdue subjects to the table of public discourse on a wide scale. Rhetorical empathy can, however, be used productively along with other forms of engagement, especially in order to sustain social movements (and the people within them).

Biologist Frans de Waal argues in *The Age of Empathy* that empathy is part of the evolutionary process: we need to put others first at times in order to perpetuate the community. Whatever the origin of our desires for connection and peace, and despite its challenges and constraints, there is merit to the idea that a peaceful rhetoric begets peaceful rhetoric. The practice of nonviolent rhetoric, pronounced in examples such as Nelson Mandela and Martin Luther King Jr., figures prominently in feminist rhetorical theories. Nonviolent, empathetic practices, foundational to a variety of spiritual and religious traditions, are motivating factors in the rhetoric of Addams and Lee.

More work on engaging across difference is needed in rhetorical theory and the field of writing studies, particularly cross-disciplinary work with fields such as social and cognitive psychology. Design thinking represents one such way in which scholars from a range of disciplines are collaborating around innovative approaches to community-based, empathetic problem solving and design.[6] I hope this book will encourage more research on examples of engagement across difference—on, for example, nonprofit groups such as Narrative 4 and journalists such as Van Jones, who are working to promote greater understanding between polarized groups. These examples may be the exception—they certainly resist the practice of media outlets featuring conflict stories to get ratings—but they should be highlighted as possibilities. We need models, and we need more theories that explain how rhetoric can help bring people together rather than dividing us.

Closer to home, it would be interesting to see longitudinal, qualitative studies that follow students across their time in college, tracing their changes in attitude on polarizing subjects and people different from them and particularly how these changes may be reflected in their writing. Along the same lines, a helpful way of countering the larger discourse around credible news sources may be to recast citation practices as ways of engaging across difference using approaches such as rhetorical empathy, adding to the valuable work Rebecca Moore Howard and Sandra Jamieson have done with the Citation Project.[7]

* * *

I end by returning to where I started: How can a peace-based, supremely feminist, antiracist practice such as empathy have any impact in our culture? How can we teach writing and ethical rhetorical engagement in the midst of tremendous polarization? What are the implications of this research for rhetorical theory and for us as teachers and as human beings?

Rhetorical empathy offers a way of seeing and being in the world and with others that has implications for almost every single encounter and problem we face in our daily lives. The way of thinking we've inherited from Aristotelian logic and hierarchies influences how we approach people and problems in the West. It's not that there is a Western way of thinking and an Eastern way of thinking; in fact, thinking in terms of opposites and pitting them against one another is characteristic of the way of thinking in which we've been immersed. It's difficult if not impossible to get outside our own thinking and to think about how we think, which is why comparative rhetoric and practices such as reflexive inquiry described by Qualley are so important. The way of thinking represented by the yin yang symbol suggests that instead of trying to overcome other ideas in order to verify our own, or trying to overcome differences by transcending them, we see difference—and the Other—as part of ourselves. In this way of thinking, we embrace difference. We learn from it. This process is hard and painful—there's no way around that. But in this process, we also must embrace the lesson of feminist rhetorical theory: power and the body are always present in any way of thinking. The lack of focus on the body and the material consequences of our philosophies may, for example, help explain why there can be wonderfully egalitarian theories about differences working together within Confucian-influenced cultures and yet women continue to hold less value than men in those cultures. Patriarchal, racist, colonialist, and homophobic thinking is embedded in every major philosophical system. Thinking with rhetorical empathy does not mean that we ignore or do not address oppression and power imbalances but that we address them differently; we resist using the practices and ways of thinking we're resisting. In trying to protest the misuse of power, we can't fall prey to the trap of becoming the thing we resist.

Rhetorical empathy has limits; it has considerable challenges. It is far from perfect and isn't always the best choice. It does, however, offer pragmatic ways of bridging difference—not erasing it but seeing it as productive—and of teaching our students to do the same. It involves the use of story as a way of knowing and a way of inviting others to understand what motivates us, and in turn it becomes a way for us as interlocutors to listen rhetorically by being open to the emotions and changes that occur in this process.

In reflecting on the uses of rhetorical empathy in a polarized age, it may be useful also to think about what rhetorical empathy is not:

It is not getting the last word.

It is not (only) proving we're right.

It is not listening to someone (only) to jump in to get our point across.

It *is* taking in the stories of others as vital parts of their identity and motivations.

It is acknowledging how our own stories play an ongoing role in how we write and engage with others on a moment-by-moment basis.

It is, in many ways, a form of love. It is empathy for ourselves and, in turn, for others.[8]

What would rhetorical empathy look like in our everyday lives, in our close relationships with friends and family and with the people we deal with on a weekly basis who make us shake our heads with near desperation? What about empathy for ourselves (which a dear, late mentor and friend taught me can be the hardest kind)? What would it look like in our teaching and with our students? In our research, as we consider which scholars to read and cite and try to understand and engage with?

Adopting the topos of empathy as a way of being-with-others offers possibilities for seeing in new ways. It creates openings for rhetorical engagement to occur and, more important, for it to continue. The rhetors and writers in this project not only use rhetorical empathy as a way of engaging with others, they embody it. Empathy becomes more than a "strategy;" it's a way of life that forms a vital part of their identity. They choose peace even in the midst of the struggle, working for a more ethical, better version of themselves and their world.

NOTES

INTRODUCTION: CHANGING THE SUBJECT

1. Welty, "Where," 24–25.
2. Welty, "Firing."
3. Welty, *On Writing*, 95.
4. The definition of the Other is slippery, always changing depending on our rhetorical situation and which of our intersectional identities we find at the forefront at any particular time. A defining characteristic of rhetorical empathy is how the Other is constructed by a rhetor.
   For the most extensive study on empathy and literature, see Keen, *Empathy and the Novel*.
5. Obama and Robinson, "President Obama."
6. I rely on Aristotle's notion of topoi in *On Rhetoric*, signifying a "place" or common way of thinking from which we invent arguments, often thought of as a stance or attitude, and I use *trope* to signify a rhetorical and discursive "product" of such a stance or way of thinking.
7. Hoffman, *Empathy*.
8. Eisenberg and Strayer, *Empathy*, 3–5.
9. Wispé, "History," 17.
10. Fleckenstein, 715.
11. Eisenberg and Strayer.
12. Wispé, "The Distinction," 318.
13. Lindquist, "Class," 197.
14. Lindquist, 197.
15. Lindquist, 197.
16. Lindquist, 198.
17. Lindquist, 198.
18. Lindquist, 202.
19. Lindquist, 202–3.
20. Lindquist, 204.
21. Roskelly and Ronald, *Reason*; Ritchie and Ronald, "Introduction," xxvii.
22. Qualley, *Turns*; Yancey, *Rhetoric*.
23. Lynch, "Rhetorics."
24. Ricoeur, *Freud*; Jurecic, "Empathy," 16.
25. Ratcliffe, *Rhetorical*, 72.
26. Lynch, "Rhetorics," 20.
27. Lynch, 7.
28. Lynch, 10.
29. Aristotle, *On Rhetoric*, 2.8.12–15.
30. See "*Eleos*" / Ἔλεος in Vine and Bruce, *Vine's Expository Dictionary*.
31. Mao, *Reading*.

32. BBC Trending, "'I Am Housemaid, Hear Me Roar,'" BBC News, August 1, 2016, http://www.bbc.com/news/blogs-trending-36927502.

33. Duffy, "Virtuous."

CHAPTER 1: A BRIEF HISTORY OF EMPATHY

1. Christophersen, "Obama's."
2. Garrett, "Obama.'"
3. Garrett.
4. Shapiro, "Sotomayor."
5. Since the concept of empathy as we know it did not exist until the late nineteenth century, I also explore the circulation of concepts such as pity, sympathy, and compassion.
6. Mao, *Reading*.
7. Definitions of empathy, sympathy, compassion, pity, and similar concepts vary widely between and within disciplines such as rhetoric, communication, psychology, philosophy, and neurosciences.
8. Kennedy, *Comparative*, 98.
9. Kennedy, 198.
10. According to Xiaoye You, scholars in comparative rhetoric have complicated the notion that rhetoric within Chinese rhetorical traditions leans toward indirect approaches focused on maintaining harmony, yet Kennedy's analysis points to elements within discourse beyond the Euro-American tradition in which such approaches are importantly present, in Hall and Ames's terms.
11. Hall and Ames, *Anticipating*, xv.
12. Jarratt, *Rereading*, 65.
13. Lloyd, "Rethinking," 375.
14. Lu, *Rhetoric*, 291.
15. Hall and Ames, *Anticipating*, 209.
16. Peng and Nisbett, "Culture," 741.
17. Solomon, "Cross-Cultural," 276.
18. Lyon, "Confucian," 136.
19. Davis, *Inessential*, 14.
20. Davis, 14.
21. Diab, *Shades*, 5.
22. Diab, 31.
23. Diab, 26.
24. Diab, 27.
25. Diab, 11.
26. Diab, 12.
27. Diab, 16.
28. Diab, 18.
29. Diab, 18.
30. Mao, "Doing," 64–69.
31. Aristotle, *On Rhetoric*, 124.

32. I refer to Keen (6) for commonplaces surrounding empathy as emblematic of the human but stress the problematic nature of such commonplaces, as noted by Melanie Yergeau in *Authoring Autism.*
33. Aristotle, *On Rhetoric,* 2.8.4–7.
34. Aristotle, 2.8.12–15.
35. Aristotle associates appeals based on *eleos* to acting (154), referring in this context to the *hypokrisis:* "Necessarily those are more pitiable who contribute to the effect by gestures and cries and display of feelings and generally in their acting [*hypokrisis*]." The association of empathy with manipulation and acting relates to the distinction between *surface empathy* and *deep empathy* Julie Lindquist appropriates in her discussion of strategic empathy.
36. Luke 10:27 (King James Bible).
37. Luke 10:30–37 (King James Bible).
38. Confucius, *Analects,* 15.24.
39. Hall and Ames, *Anticipating,* 199.
40. Corbett, "Rhetoric," 288–89.
41. Campbell, *Philosophy,* 1.
42. Campbell, 76.
43. Campbell, 76.
44. Hume defines and uses sympathy as feeling with rather than what we think of as pity or feeling for and is, I argue, closer to current significations of empathy.
45. Hume does not use the term *concentric circles* but rather discusses "the diminuation of sympathy by the separation of relations" (2.1.11).
46. Bacon's theory of discourse and the role of rhetoric was based on the concept of faculty psychology, which constructed the mind as a collection of sections, each of which served a certain function, including understanding, reason, imagination, memory, appetite, and will (Zappan, 61). Faculty psychology bears a striking resemblance to current research in cognitive science in which empathetic responses are located in the prefontal cortex of the brain (Shamay-Tsoory, Aharon Peretz, and Perry).
47. Hume, *Treatise,* 2.3.3.
48. Hume, 2.1.11, sec. 8.
49. Vine and Bruce, "*Eleos*" / Ἔλεος.
50. Vischer, *Empathy,* 109.
51. Mallgrave and Ikonomou, "Introduction," 17.
52. Vischer, *Empathy,* 1.
53. Vischer, 25.
54. Vischer, 105.
55. Vischer, 109.
56. Wispé, "History," 21.
57. Keen, *Empathy,* 39.
58. Wispé, "History," 25.
59. Freud, *Civilization,* 13.
60. Freud, 11.
61. Rogers, *On Becoming,* 331.
62. Burke, *Rhetoric,* 43.

63.   I'm oversimplifying Young, Becker, and Pike's work, which unfortunately
      can result when an important theory is unmoored from its original con-
      text and reproduced in textbooks.
64.   Booth, *Rhetoric*, 50.
65.   Booth, 76.
66.   Flower, "Talking," 44.
67.   Flower, 44.
68.   Flower, 47.
69.   Flower, 49.
70.   McComiskey, *Dialectical*, 3.
71.   McComiskey, 4.
72.   Jarratt, *Rereading*, 68–69.
73.   Ritchie and Ronald, "Introduction," 211.
74.   Buck, "Present," 214.
75.   Foss and Griffin, "Beyond," 2.
76.   Foss and Griffin, 3.
77.   Ritchie and Ronald, "Introduction," xvi.
78.   Royster and Kirsch, *Feminist*, 4.
79.   Royster and Kirsch, 3.
80.   Adler-Kassner, *Activist*, 168.
81.   Adler-Kassner, 27.
82.   Benhabib, *Situating*.
83.   These features of Benhabib's "public sphere of the generalized other"
      are characteristic of modern rhetorical theories such as Rogerian rheto-
      ric, which see the Other as an equal without fully taking into account
      power differentials.
84.   Benhabib, *Situating*, 286.
85.   Benhabib, 12.
86.   Gilligan's theory focuses on the intervention of women's experiences
      into theories of moral development that had, until the time of the
      publication of *In a Different Voice* (1982), focused on the experiences of
      middle- to upper-middle-class males. She argues for an epistemology
      based on connectedness and experience (an "ethic of care") rather than
      generalized principles (an "ethic of justice") (173).
87.   Vetlesen, *Perception*, 18.
88.   Vetlesen, 9.
89.   Hume uses the term *sympathy*, although his account of the function of
      sympathy is similar to how I conceive of empathy's function in terms of
      its connection to ethical reasoning.

CHAPTER 2: THREADS OF FEMINIST
RHETORICAL PRACTICES

1.   Addams, "Domestic," 626–31; Addams, "Belated," 536–50.
      Addams spoke on a Friday morning at ten o'clock, delivering a fairly
      brief address, a summary of which, entitled "Domestic Service and the

Family Claim," was published in the proceedings of the congress. A fuller version of her arguments, three times the length of her speech in the congress proceedings, was published three years later in the *American Journal of Sociology* and titled "A Belated Industry." For the purposes of analysis, I use the article-length version of her speech, as full contents of her Columbian Exposition speech is included within the "Belated Industry" article.

2. The Women's Congress was held in what is now the Art Institute of Chicago, which was built specifically for the world's fair and only one of two buildings (the Field Museum the other) that survives; the rest of the two hundred temporary structures constructed for the fair burned to the ground during the Pullman Strike the next summer.

3. Polanyi, *Personal*; Keller, *Feeling*.

4. Stanton, *Eighty Years*, 139.

5. Dudden, *Serving*, 187-88.

6. Knight, *Citizen*, 391.

7. Addams, *Twenty*, 393.

8. Stigler, *Domestic*, 5.

9. Katzman, *Seven*, 5.

    A notable example of an ethnographic exposé on working-class conditions written by an educated member of the middle class is Lillian Pettengill's *Toilers of the Home* (1902), a precursor of work such as Barbara Ehrenreich's *Nickel and Dimed: On (Not) Getting by in America* (2001). Pettengill was a graduate of Mount Holyoke who in the late 1890s was unable to find employment as a journalist and so went to work as a live-in domestic servant for one year, partly to pay the bills and have a roof over her head and partly as a participant-observer researcher. Katzman calls her monograph on her experience one of the most extensive accounts of a domestic worker in the United States during the late Gilded Age.

10. Ritchie and Ronald, "Introduction," xxviii.

11. Lu, *Rhetoric*; Lipson and Binkley, "Introduction."

    I resist the separation of rhetoric and philosophy common in the Euro-American intellectual tradition. Scholars of comparative rhetoric such as Lu and Lipson and Binkley have pointed out that in rhetoric beyond the Western canon, rhetoric and philosophy were not separated to the extent they have been in the Greek/Aristotelian tradition.

12. Knight, *Citizen*, 192. The College Settlement Association (CSA), comprised of women educated at the seven-sister colleges (Smith, Wellesley, Vassar, Bryn Mawr, Mount Holyoke, Radcliffe, and Barnard) established a settlement house in New York City two weeks after Hull House opened.

13. Knight, 170.

14. Addams, "Belated," 536.

15. Dudden, *Serving*.

16. Dudden, 7.

17. Dudden, 46.

18. Dudden, 54.

19. Addams, "Belated," 543.

20. Addams, 543.

21. Addams, 548.
22. Addams, 548.
23. Dudden, *Serving,* 4.
24. Addams, "Belated," 547.
25. Addams, 547.
26. Addams, 547.
27. "'Preto' or 'Negro'?"
28. Urban Dictionary, s.v. "rara," https://www.urbandictionary.com/define.php?term=Rara.
29. Gries, "Introduction," 3–26.
30. Ansari and Almasy, "Lochte."
31. Garcia-Navarro, "Photos."
32. "Q&A"
33. Loveman, Muniz, and Bailey, "Brazil?," 12.
34. Lauderdale Graham, *House.*
35. International Labour Office, *Domestic,* 24.
36. International Labour Office, 26.
37. BBC Trending, "I Am Housemaid."
38. Sheridan, Ridolfo, and Michel, *Available.*
39. Turkle, *Reclaiming.*

CHAPTER 3: RHETORICAL EMPATHY IN THE GAY-RIGHTS/RELIGIOUS DIVIDE

1. Examples of other guest bloggers who engaged in discursive question-and-answer forums in the series include a pagan, a Catholic, a Mormon, a Seventh-Day Adventist, a feminist, an atheist, and a transgender woman.
2. Crowley, *Toward,* 69.
3. While Crowley's characterization of fundamentalists rings true in many respects, and while she concedes that liberal Christians do exist, she does not identify people or groups within the ranks of the large umbrella she calls "fundamentalist" who are actively working for change within their own communities. The one exception she notes (9) is the social justice, Left-leaning Christian group Sojourners, founded by Jim Wallis in 1971. Within the larger umbrella of the Christian right, Crowley conflates fundamentalists and evangelicals—understandable given the way the terms *religious Right, Christian Right, fundamentalists,* and *evangelicals* circulate synonymously in public discourse and the media. Her conflation, however, of fundamentalist and evangelical Christians has the unfortunate consequence of reducing one of the largest religious blocs in the United States to a homogenous group. As Crowley points out, religious historian George Marsden calls a fundamentalist an "evangelical who is mad about something" (103). One of my points of departure from Crowley is that in terms of actual beliefs, fundamentalists are a small group in the United States compared to evangelicals.
4. Crowley, *Toward,* 189.
5. Public Religion Research Institute, "How Social."

6. Crowley, *Toward*, 192–94.
7. Crowley, 194.
8. Public Religion Research Institute, "Majority."
9. Geiger, "Unpredictable," 249.
10. Rachel Held Evans, "Ask a Gay Christian . . . (Response)," September 19, 2011, http://rachelheldevans.com/ask-a-gay-christian-response.
11. Held Evans.
12. Held Evans.
13. Held Evans.
14. Held Evans.
15. Justin Lee, email interview with the author, December 9, 2011.
16. Decety and Meyer, "From Emotion," 1074.
17. Adler-Kassner, *Activist*, 29.
18. Addams, "A Modern Lear," 168. I owe Kate Ronald a debt for her work analyzing Jane Addams's use of the term "affectionate interpretation." See Ronald, "Philanthropy as Interpretation."
19. Brown, "Peacemaking," 781.
20. Brown, 794.
21. Brown, 798, citing Gabriella Blum and Robert H. Mnookin, "When Not to Negotiate," in *The Negotiator's Fieldbook: The Desk Reference for the Experienced Negotiator*, edited by Andrea Kupfer Schneider and Christopher Honeyman (Washington, DC: American Bar Association, 2006).
22. Held Evans.
23. Lee, email interview with author, December 9, 2011.
24. Lee.
25. Lee.
26. Held Evans.
27. Held Evans.

CHAPTER 4: BEYOND "COMMON GROUND"

1. Goldblatt, "Don't," 441.
2. Goldblatt, 442.
3. Campbell, *Philosophy*, 1.
4. I use *persuasion* and *argument* interchangeably, both representing the idea that rhetoric's purpose is to change an audience's mind for one's own ends.
5. Lynch et al., "Moments," 84.
6. Jarratt, "Feminism," 263–80. Originally published in Patricia Harkin and John Schlib, eds., *Contending with Words: Composition and Rhetoric in a Postmodern Age* (New Yok: MLA, 1991), 105–24.
7. Jarratt, "Feminism," 270.
8. Lynch, George, and Cooper, "Moments," 68.
9. In *Rhetoric: Discovery and Change*, Young, Becker, and Pike write that "when the writer builds bridges he [*sic*] must accept the possibility that he, as well as his reader, may be changed. Of course, he may use rhetorical techniques to manipulate others for his own ends, seeking to change

them while insulating himself from ideas that might force changes in his own mind. . . . But if the writer seeks to establish a true community by means of his words, he himself must be willing to change" (178).

10. Lynch, George, and Cooper, "Moments," 68.
11. Adler-Kassner, *Activist*, 32.
12. See Keller, *Feeling*, a biography of cytogeneticist Barbara McClintock (1902–1992), who believed the most valuable scientific epistemology is grounded in "a feeling for the organism," or personal interaction with the object of study to the point that the object has value and meaning beyond its utilitarian use.
13. See Excelsior College's Online Writing Lab, https://owl.excelsior.edu/argument-and-critical-thinking/argumentative-purposes/argumentative-purposes-narrative/.
14. Reid, "Teaching," W198.
15. Qualley, *Turns*, 39.
16. Qualley, 11.
17. Qualley, 11.
18. Qualley, 37.
19. See Belenky et al.'s work that challenges William G. Perry's theories of cognitive development in terms of content and, maybe more importantly, methodology. Perry uses male undergraduates at Harvard as research subjects, while Belenky and colleagues focus on women outside academic environments from a variety of ethnicities, social classes, and education levels. They argue that women's experiences and socialization lead them to form knowledge in different ways than men. One of the ways is what they call connected knowing, which emphasizes context, understanding an Other's point of view, and personal experience rather than detached objectivity and critical analysis.
20. In "Feminist Responses to Rogerian Argument," Phyllis Lassner argues that a Rogerian approach requires a detached writing style and unemotional description of opposing views. She describes a women's studies class in which she used Maxine Hairston's textbook based on Rogerian rhetoric. She initially was excited about using the text because she believed in the principles it advocated but was disappointed when the majority of her female students found the approach repressive and difficult. She explains that "they needed to figure out how to be comfortable in the role of 'an equal' in relation to those on the other side of the issues who had failed to regard them as such" (225). Her essay raises the question of whether it's fair or even possible to ask someone who has been marginalized to suspend judgments, assume neutrality, and empathize with the very ones who have perpetuated their condition.

EPILOGUE: A THEORY OF RHETORICAL EMPATHY

1. See Knight, *Citizen*, for a definitive biography of Addams.
2. Putnam, *American*, 542–46.

3.   Phelps-Roper, "I Grew Up."
4.   Chen, "Unfollow."
5.   See Schlib, *Rhetorical Refusals.*
6.   Wible, "Getting"; Gardner, "Can Design?" For an overview see Plattner, Meinel, and Leifer, *Design Thinking.*
7.   See the Citation Project website for details and a list of related publications at http://www.citationproject.net/publications/.
8.   I thank Michele Eodice for the practice of thinking through what something is by considering what it is not, especially in her piece "Participatory Hospitality and Writing Centers."

REFERENCES

Addams, Jane. "A Belated Industry." *American Journal of Sociology* 1, no. 5 (March 1896): 536–50.

Addams, Jane. "Domestic Service and the Family Claim." In *The World's Congress of Representative Women* Vol. 2, edited by Mary Wright Sewell, 626–31. Chicago: Rand, McNally, 1894.

Addams, Jane. *The Long Road of Woman's Memory.* New York: Macmillan, 1916.

Addams, Jane. "A Modern Lear." In *The Jane Addams Reader,* edited by Jean Bethke Elshtain. New York: Basic Books, 2002.

Addams, Jane. *Twenty Years at Hull-House.* New York: Signet, 1961.

Adler-Kassner, Linda. *The Activist WPA: Changing Stories about Writing and Writers.* Logan: Utah State University Press, 2008.

Ahmed, Sara. *The Cultural Politics of Emotion.* New York: Routledge, 2004.

Ansari, Azadeh, and Steve Almasy. "Lochte: 'I Over-Exaggerated' Robbery Story." CNN, August 22, 2016. http://www.cnn.com/2016/08/20/sport/us-olym pics-swimmers-reported-robbery-future/index.html.

Aristotle. *On Rhetoric: A Theory of Civic Discourse.* Translated by George A. Kennedy. New York: Oxford University Press, 1991.

Barna Group. "Spiritual Profile of Homosexual Adults Provides Surprising Insights." Barna.org. June 22, 2009. https://www.barna.com/research/spiritual -profile-of-homosexual-adults-provides-surprising-insights/.

Battiste, Marie. *Decolonizing Education.* Vancouver: Purich, 2013.

Beecher, Catharine Esther, and Harriet Beecher Stowe. *The American Woman's Home: Or Principles of Domestic Science.* New York: J. B. Ford and Company, 1869.

Belenky, Mary Field, Blythe McVicker Clinchy, Nancy Rule Goldberger, and Jill Mattuck Tarule. *Women's Ways of Knowing: The Development of Self, Voice, and Mind.* New York: Basic Books, 1997.

Benhabib, Selya. "Introduction: The Democratic Moment and the Problem of Difference." In *Democracy and Difference: Contesting the Boundaries of the Political,* edited by Seyla Benhabib. Princeton, NJ: Princeton University Press, 1996.

Benhabib, Selya. *Situating the Self: Gender, Community, and Postmodernism in Contemporary Ethics.* London: Routledge, 1992.

Berlant, Lauren. *The Female Complaint: The Unfinished Business of Sentimentality in American Culture.* Durham, NC: Duke University Press, 2008.

Booth, Wayne. *The Rhetoric of Rhetoric: The Quest for Effective Communication.* Malden, MA: Blackwell, 2004.

Brown, Jennifer Gerarda. "Peacemaking in the Culture War between Gay Rights and Religious Liberty." *Iowa Law Review* 95 (2010): 747–819.

Buck, Gertrude. "The Present Status of Rhetorical Theory." In *Available Means: An Anthology of Women's Rhetoric(s),* edited by Joy Ritchie and Kate Ronald, 212–18. Pittsburgh: University of Pittsburgh Press, 2001.

DOI: 10.7330/9781607329107.c006

Burke, Kenneth. *A Rhetoric of Motives.* Berkeley: University of California Press, 1950.

Butler, Judith. *Precarious Life: The Power of Mourning and Violence.* New York: Verso, 2004.

Campbell, George. *The Philosophy of Rhetoric.* Edited by Lloyd Bitzer. Carbondale: Southern Illinois University Press, 1963.

Chen, Adrian. "Unfollow: How a Prized Daughter of the Westboro Baptist Church Came to Question its Beliefs" *New Yorker,* November 23, 2015. https://www.newyorker.com/magazine/2015/11/23/conversion-via-twitter-westboro-baptist-church-megan-phelps-roper.

Christophersen, James. "Obama's Empathy Rule: Alive and Well in the Second Term." *National Review,* April 9, 2013.

Coleman, Peter T. *The Five Percent: Finding Solutions to Seemingly Impossible Conflicts.* New York: Public Affairs, 2011.

Confucius. *The Analects of Confucius: A Philosophical Translation.* Translated by Robert T. Ames and Henry Rosemont Jr. New York: Ballantine, 1998.

Corbett, Edward P. J. "The Rhetoric of the Open Hand and the Rhetoric of the Closed Fist." *College Composition and Communication* 20, no. 5 (December 1969): 288–96.

Corder, Jim. "What I Learned at School." *College Composition and Communication* 26, no. 4 (December 1975): 330–34.

Crowley, Sharon. *Toward a Civil Discourse: Rhetoric and Fundamentalism.* Pittsburgh: University of Pittsburgh Press, 2006.

Davis, Diane. *Inessential Solidarity: Rhetoric and Foreigner Relations.* Pittsburgh: University of Pittsburgh Press, 2010.

Decety, Jean, and Phillip Jackson. "The Functional Architecture of Human Empathy." *Behavioral and Cognitive Neuroscience Reviews* 3, no. 2 (2004): 71–100.

Decety, Jean, and Meghan Meyer. "From Emotion Resonance to Empathic Understanding: A Social Developmental Neuroscience Account." *Development and Psychopathology* 20, no. 4 (2008): 1053–80.

DeStigter, Todd. "Public Displays of Affection: Political Community through Critical Empathy." *Research in the Teaching of English* 33 (1999): 235–44.

de Waal, Frans. *The Age of Empathy: Nature's Lessons for a Kinder Society.* New York: Three Rivers Press, 2009.

Diab, Rasha. *Shades of Ṣulḥ: The Rhetorics of Arab-Islamic Reconciliation.* Pittsburgh: University of Pittsburgh Press, 2016.

Dudden, Faye E. *Serving Women: Household Service in Nineteenth-Century America.* Middletown, CT: Wesleyan University Press, 1985.

Duffy, John. "Virtuous Arguments." *Inside Higher Ed,* March 16, 2012.

Ehrenreich, Barbara. *Nickel and Dimed: On (Not) Getting By in America.* New York: Henry Holt and Company, 2001.

Eisenberg, Nancy, and Janet Strayer. *Empathy and Its Development.* Cambridge: Cambridge University Press, 1987.

Eodice, Michele. "Participatory Hospitality in Writing Centers." In *The Rhetoric of Participation,* edited by Paige V. Banaji, Lisa Blankenship, Katherine DeLuca, Lauren Obermark, and Ryan Omizo. Logan: Computers and Composition Digital Press/Utah State University Press, 2019.

Eodice, Michele, Anne Ellen Geller, and Neal Lerner. *The Meaningful Writing Project: Learning, Teaching, and Writing in Higher Education.* Logan: Utah State University Press, 2016.

Fairclough, Norman. *Language and Power.* New York: Longman, 1989.

Fernandes, Joyce. 2016. "Eu, Empregada Doméstica." Facebook. https://www.facebook.com/euempregadadomestica/.

Fisher, Walter R. "Narration as a Human Communication Paradigm: The Case of Public Moral Argument." *Communication Monographs* 51, no. 1 (June 2009): 1–22. doi: 10.1080/03637758409390180.

Fleckenstein, Kristie S. "Once Again with Feeling: Empathy in Deliberative Discourse." *JAC* 27, nos. 3/4 (2007): 701–16.

Flower, Linda. "Talking across Difference: Intercultural Rhetoric and the Search for Situated Knowledge." *College Communication and Composition* 55, no. 1 (Sept. 2003): 38-68.

Foss, Sonja K., and Cindy L. Griffin. "Beyond Persuasion: A Proposal for an Invitational Rhetoric." *Communication Monographs* 62, no. 1 (1995): 2–18.

Fraser, Nancy. "Rethinking the Public Sphere: A Contribution to the Critique of Actually Existing Democracy." *Social Text* 25, no. 26 (1990): 56–80.

Freud, Sigmund. *Civilization and Its Discontents.* New York: Norton, 1961.

Fuss, Diana. *Identification Papers: Readings on Psychoanalysis, Sexuality, and Culture.* New York: Routledge, 1995.

Garcia-Navarro, Lulu. "Photos Reveal Harsh Detail of Brazil's History with Slavery." NPR, November 12, 2013. https://www.npr.org/sections/parallels/2013/11/12/244563532/photos-reveal-harsh-detail-of-brazils-history-with-slavery.

Gardner, Lee. "Can Design Thinking Redesign Higher Ed?" *Chronicle of Higher Education,* September 10, 2017. http://universityinnovationfellows.org/wp-content/uploads/2015/08/Can-Design-Thinking-Redesign-Higher-Ed_-The-Chronicle-of-Higher-Education.pdf.

Garrett, Major. "Obama Pushes for 'Empathetic Supreme Court Justices.'" Fox News, May 1, 2009. http://www.foxnews.com/politics/2009/05/01/obama-pushes-empathetic-supreme-court-justices.html.

Geiger, T. J. "Unpredictable Encounters: Religious Discourse, Sexuality, and the Free Exercise of Rhetoric." *College English* 75, no. 3 (January 2013): 248–69.

Gilligan, Carol. *In a Different Voice: Psychological Theory and Women's Development.* Cambridge, MA: Harvard University Press, 1982.

Gilman, Charlotte Perkins. *What Diantha Did.* Durham, NC: Duke University Press, 2005.

Goldblatt, Eli. "Don't Call It Expressivism: Legacies of a 'Tacit' Tradition." *College Composition and Communication* 68, no. 3 (February 2017): 438–65.

Gries, Laurie E. "Introduction: Circulation as an Emerging Threshold Concept." In *Circulation, Writing, and Rhetoric.* Logan: Utah State University Press, 2018.

Gross, Daniel. *The Secret History of Emotion.* Chicago: University of Chicago Press, 2006.

Hall, David L., and Roger T. Ames. *Anticipating China: Thinking through the Narratives of Chinese and Western Culture.* Albany: SUNY Press, 1995.

Heidegger, Martin. *Being and Time.* Translated by John Macquarries and Edward Robinson. New York: Harper and Row, 1962.

Hochschild, Arlie Russell. *Strangers in Their Own Land: Anger and Mourning on the American Right.* New York: The New Press, 2016.

Hoffman, Martin. *Empathy and Moral Development: Implications for Caring and Justice.* Cambridge: Cambridge University Press, 2000.

Hume, David. *A Treatise of Human Nature.* Oxford: Clarendon, 1964. First published in 1740.

International Labour Office. *Domestic Workers across the World: Global and Regional Statistics and the Extent of Legal Protection.* International Labour Office: Geneva, 2013. http://www.ilo.org/wcmsp5/groups/public/—dgreports/ —dcomm/—publ/documents/publication/wcms_173363.pdf.

Jarratt, Susan C. "Feminism and Composition: The Case for Conflict." In *Feminism and Composition: A Critical Sourcebook,* edited by Gesa E. Kirsch, Faye Spender Maor, Lance Massey, Lee Nickoson-Massey, and Mary P. Sheridan-Rabideau, 263–80. New York: Bedford/St. Martin's, 2003.

Jarratt, Susan C. *Rereading the Sophists: Classical Rhetoric Refigured.* Carbondale: Southern Illinois University Press, 1991.

Jurecic, Ann. "Empathy and the Critic." *College English* 74, no. 1 (September 2011): 10–27.

Katzman, David M. *Seven Days a Week: Women and Domestic Service in Industrializing America.* New York: Oxford University Press, 1978.

Keen, Susan. *Empathy and the Novel.* New York: Oxford University Press, 2007.

Keller, Evelyn Fox. *A Feeling for the Organism: The Life and Work of Barbara McClintock.* New York: Henry Holt, 2003.

Kennedy, George. *Comparative Rhetoric: An Historical and Cross-Cultural Introduction.* New York: Cambridge, 1997.

Kinneavy, James L. *A Theory of Discourse.* Englewood Cliffs, NJ: Prentice Hall, 1971.

Knight, Louise W. *Citizen: Jane Addams and the Struggle for Democracy.* Chicago: University of Chicago Press, 2005.

Knoblauch, A. Abby. "A Textbook Argument: Definitions of Argument in Leading Composition Textbooks." *College Composition and Communication* 63, no. 2 (December 2011): 244–68.

Lassner, Phyllis. "Feminist Responses to Rogerian Rhetoric." *Rhetoric Review* 8, no. 2 (Spring 1990): 220–32.

Lauderdale Graham, Sandra. *House and Street: The Domestic World of Servants and Masters in Nineteenth-Century Rio de Janeiro.* New York: Cambridge University Press, 1988.

Leake, Eric Wallace. *In the Words of Another: On the Promises and Paradoxes of Rhetorics of Empathy.* PhD diss., University of Louisville, 2011. Ann Arbor: ProQuest/UMI. (Publication No. 912748832).

Lerner, Gerda. *The Creation of Patriarchy.* New York: Oxford University Press, 1986.

Levinas, Emmanuel. *Totality and Infinity: An Essay on Exteriority.* Translated by Alphonso Lingis. Pittsburgh: Duquesne University Press, 1961.

Lindquist, Julie. "Class Affects, Classroom Affectations: Working through the Paradoxes of Strategic Empathy." *College English* 67, no. 2 (2004): 187–209.

Lipson, Carol S., and Roberta A. Binkley. "Introduction." In *Rhetoric before and beyond the Greeks,* edited by Carol S. Lipson and Roberta A. Binkley. Albany: SUNY Press, 2004.

Lloyd, Keith. "Rethinking Rhetoric from an Indian Perspective: Implications in the *Nyaya Sutra*." *Rhetoric Review* 26, no. 4 (September 2007): 365–84.

Lorde, Audre. *Sister Outsider*. Freedom, CA: The Crossing Press, 1984.

Loveman, Mara, Jeronimo O. Muniz, and Stanley R. Bailey. "Brazil in Black and White? Race Categories, the Census, and the Study of Inequality." *Ethnic and Racial Studies* 35, no. 8 (August 2012): 1–18.

Lu, Xing. *Rhetoric in Ancient China, Fifth to Third Century B.C.E.: A Comparison with Classical Greek Rhetoric*. Columbia: University of South Carolina Press, 1998.

Lunsford, Andrea A. "Aristotelian vs. Rogerian Argument: A Reassessment." *College Composition and Communication* 30, no. 2 (May 1979): 146–51.

Lunsford, Andrea A., ed. *Reclaiming Rhetorica: Women in the Rhetorical Tradition*. Pittsburgh: University of Pittsburgh Press, 1995.

Lunsford, Andrea A., and Lisa S. Ede. "On Distinctions between Classical and Modern Rhetoric." In *Essays on Classical Rhetoric and Modern Discourse*, edited by Robert J. Connors, Lisa S. Ede, and Andrea A. Lunsford. 37–50. Carbondale: Southern Illinois University Press, 1984.

Lynch, Dennis A. "Rhetorics of Proximity: Empathy in Temple Grandin and Cornel West." *Rhetoric Society Quarterly* 28, no. 1 (Winter 1998): 5–23.

Lynch, Dennis A., Diana George, and Marilyn M. Cooper. "Moments of Argument: Agonistic Inquiry and Confrontational Cooperation." *College Composition and Communication* 48, no. 1 (February 1997): 61–85.

Lyon, Arabella. "Confucian Silence and Remonstration: A Basis for Deliberation?" In *Rhetoric before and beyond the Greeks*, edited by Carol Lipson and Roberta A. Binkley, 131–46. Albany: SUNY Press, 2004.

Mallgrave, Harry Francis, and Eleftherios Ikonomou. "Introduction." In *Empathy, Form, and Space: Problems in German Aesthetics, 1873–1893*, edited by Harry F. Mallgrave and Eleftherios Ikonomou. Santa Monica, CA: Getty Center for the History of Art and the Humanities, 1994.

Mao, LuMing. "Doing Comparative Rhetoric Responsibly." *Rhetoric Society Quarterly* 41, no. 1 (2011): 64–69.

Mao, LuMing. *Reading Chinese Fortune Cookie: The Making of Chinese American Rhetoric*. Logan: Utah State University Press, 2006.

Mao, LuMing. "Returning to Yin and Yang: From Terms of Opposites to Interdependence-in-Difference." *Symposium: Comparative Rhetorical Studies in the New Contact Zone: Chinese Rhetoric Reimagined*, edited by C. Jan Swearingen and LuMing Mao. *College Composition and Communication* 60, no. 4 (June 2009): W45–W56.

Marsden, George. *Understanding Fundamentalism and Evangelicalism*. Grand Rapids, MI: Eerdmans, 1991.

McComiskey, Bruce. *Dialectical Rhetoric*. Logan: Utah State University Press, 2015.

Micciche, Laura R. *Doing Emotion: Rhetoric, Writing, Teaching*. Portsmouth, NH: Boynton/Cook, 2007.

Miller, Susan. *Trust in Texts: A Different History of Rhetoric*. Carbondale: Southern Illinois University Press, 2008.

Mouffe, Chantel. *The Return of the Political*. New York: Verso, 1993.

Obama, Barack, and Marilynne Robinson, "President Obama and Marilynne Robinson: A Conversation in Iowa." *New York Review of Books*, November 5,

2015. http://www.nybooks.com/articles/2015/11/05/president-obama
-marilynne-robinson-conversation/.

Peary, Alexandria. "Mindfulness, Buddhism, and Rogerian Argument." *JAEPL*
11 (Winter 2005/2006): 64–75.

Peng, Kaiping, and Richard E. Nisbett. "Culture, Dialectics, and Reasoning
about Contradiction." *American Psychologist* 54, no. 9 (September 1999):
741–54.

Pettengill, Lillian. *Toilers of the Home.* New York University Digital Library, 1902.
http://dlib.nyu.edu/undercover/toilers-home-lillian-pettengill-everybodys.

Phelps-Roper, Megan. "I Grew Up in the Westboro Baptist Church. Here's Why
I Left." Filmed February 2017 in New York City. TED video, 15:18, https://
www.ted.com/talks/megan_phelps_roper_i_grew_up_in_the_westboro
_baptist_church_here_s_why_i_left/transcript.

Plattner, Hasso, Christoph Meinel, and Larry J. Leifer, eds. *Design Thinking:
Understand, Improve, Apply.* Berlin: Springer-Verlag, 2011.

Polanyi, Michael. *Personal Knowledge.* London: Taylor and Francis, 2012.

Pough, Gwendolyn. "Empowering Rhetoric: Black Students Writing Black
Panthers." *College Composition and Communication* 53, no. 3 (2002): 466–86.

"'Preto' or 'Negro'? In Portuguese Both Mean 'Black,' but Which Term Should Be
Used to Define Black People? Ghanaian-Brazilian Man's Video on the Topic
Goes Viral." Black Women of Brazil. August 3, 2016. https://blackwomen
ofbrazil.co/in-portuguese-both-mean-black/.

Public Religion Research Institute. "How Social Contact with LGBT People
Impacts Attitudes on Policies." June 7, 2017. https://www.prri.org/spotlight
/lgbt-pride-month-social-contact-gay-lesbian-transgender-individuals/.

Public Religion Research Institute. "Majority of Americans Oppose Transgender
Bathroom Restrictions." March 10, 2017. https://www.prri.org/research/lgbt
-transgender-bathroom-discrimination-religious-liberty/.

Putnam, Robert. *American Grace: How Religion Unites and Divides Us.* New York:
Simon and Schuster, 2010.

"Q&A with Professor Henry Louis Gates Jr." PBS. November 11, 2015. http://
www.pbs.org/wnet/black-in-latin-america/featured/qa-with-professor-henry
-louis-gates-jr/164/.

Qualley, Donna. *Turns of Thought: Teaching Composition as Reflexive Inquiry.* Portsmouth: Boynton/Cook, 1997.

Ratcliffe, Krista. *Rhetorical Listening: Identification, Gender, Whiteness.* Carbondale:
Southern Illinois University Press, 2005.

Reid, E. Shelley. "Teaching Writing Teachers Writing: Difficulty, Exploration,
and Critical Reflection." *College Composition and Communication* 61, no. 2
(December 2009): W197–W221.

Richards, I. A. *The Philosophy of Rhetoric.* New York: Oxford University Press, 1936.

Richmond, Kia Jane. "The Ethics of Empathy: Making Connections in the
Writing Classroom." *JAEPL* 5 (Winter, 1999-2000): 37–46.

Ricoeur, Paul. *Freud and Philosophy: An Essay on Interpretation.* Translated by Denis
Savage. New Haven, CT: Yale University Press, 1977. First published in 1970.

Ritchie, Joy, and Kate Ronald. "Introduction." In *Available Means: An Anthology
of Women's Rhetoric(s),* edited by Joy Ritchie and Kate Ronald, xv–xxxi.
Pittsburgh: University of Pittsburgh Press, 2001.

Rogers, Carl R. *On Becoming a Person: A Therapist's View of Psychotherapy*. New York: Houghton Mifflin, 1961.

Ronald, Kate. "Philanthropy as Interpretation, Not Charity: Jane Addams's Civic Housekeeping as Another Response to the Progressive Era." In *Feminist Rhetorical Resilience*, edited by Elizabeth A. Flynn, Patricia Sotorin, and Ann Brady. Logan: Utah State University Press, 2012.

Rorty, Richard. *Contingency, Irony, and Solidarity*. Cambridge: Cambridge University Press, 1989.

Roskelly, Hephzibah, and Kate Ronald. *Reason to Believe: Romanticism, Pragmatism, and the Teaching of Writing*. New York: SUNY Press, 1998.

Royster, Jacqueline Jones. "When the First Voice You Hear Is Not Your Own." *College Composition and Communication* 47, no. 1 (1996): 29–40.

Royster, Jacqueline Jones, and Gesa E. Kirsch. *Feminist Rhetorical Practices*. Carbondale: Southern Illinois University Press, 2012.

Schlib, John. *Rhetorical Refusals: Defying Audiences' Expectations*. Carbondale: Southern Illinois University Press, 2007.

Sedgwick, Eve Kosofsky. *Touching Feeling: Affect, Pedagogy, Performativity*. Durham, NC: Duke University Press, 2003.

Shamay-Tsoory, S. G., J. Aharon-Peretz, and D. Perry. "Two Systems for Empathy: A Double Dissociation between Emotional and Cognitive Empathy in Inferior Frontal Gyrus Versus Ventromedial Prefrontal Lesions." *Brain* 132, no. 3 (March 2009): 617–27.

Shapiro, Ari. "Sotomayor Differs with Obama on 'Empathy' Issue." NPR. July 14, 2009.

Sheridan, David M., Jim Ridolfo, and Anthony J. Michel. *The Available Means of Persuasion: Mapping a Theory and Pedagogy of Multimodal Public Rhetoric*. Anderson, SC: Parlor, 2012.

Solomon, Robert. "The Cross-Cultural Comparison of Emotion." In *Emotions in Asian Thought: A Dialogue in Comparative Philosophy*, edited by Joel Marks and Roger T. Ames, 253–308. Albany: SUNY Press, 1995.

Stanton, Elizabeth Cady. *Eighty Years and More: Reminiscences 1815–1897*. New York: T. Fisher Unwin, 1898.

Stigler, George J. *Domestic Service in the United States: 1900–1940*. New York: National Bureau of Economic Research, 1946.

Teich, Nathaniel. "The Rhetoric of Empathy: Ethical Foundations of Dialogical Communication." *JAEPL* 14 (Winter 2008/2009): 12–21.

Toulmin, Stephen. *The Uses of Argument*. New York: Cambridge University Press, 2008.

Turkle, Sherry. *Reclaiming Conversation: The Power of Talk in a Digital Age*. New York: Penguin, 2015.

Vetlesen, Arne Johan. *Perception, Empathy, and Judgment: An Inquiry into the Preconditions of Moral Performance*. University Park: Penn State University Press, 1993.

Vine, W. E., and F. F. Bruce, eds. *Vine's Expository Dictionary of Old and New Testament Words*. Old Tappan, NJ: Fleming H. Revel, 1981.

Vischer, Robert. *Empathy, Form, and Space: Problems in German Aesthetics, 1873–1893*, edited by Harry F. Mallgrave and Eleftherios Ikonomou. Santa Monica, CA: Getty Center for the History of Art and the Humanities, 1994.

Welty, Eudora. "Firing Line with William F. Buckley Jr.: The Southern Imagination." Filmed on December 12, 1972. YouTube video, 59:17. Posted January 26, 2017. https://www.youtube.com/watch?v=6RoWFb2pgjE.

Welty, Eudora. *On Writing*. New York: Random House, 2002.

Welty, Eudora. "Where Is the Voice Coming From." *New Yorker*, July 6, 1963.

Wible, Scott. "Getting Students Out of the Classroom: Using Design Thinking to Teach Inquiry and Invention in the Writing Course." Keynote address at the Thomas R. Watson Symposium. Louisville, Kentucky, March 2016.

Wispé, Lauren. "The Distinction between Sympathy and Empathy: To Call Forth a Concept, a Word Is Needed." *Journal of Personality and Social Psychology* 50, no. 2 (1986): 314–21.

Wispé, Lauren. "History of the Concept of Empathy." In *Empathy and Its Development*, edited by Nancy Eisenberg and Janet Strayer, 17–37. New York: Cambridge University Press, 1987.

Yancey, Kathleen Blake, ed. *A Rhetoric of Reflection*. Logan: Utah State University Press, 2016.

Yergeau, Melanie. *Authoring Autism: On Rhetoric and Neurological Queerness*. Durham, NC: Duke University Press, 2018.

You, Xiaoye. "Confucians Love to Argue: Policy Essays in Ancient China." In *Symposium: Comparative Rhetorical Studies in the New Contact Zone: Chinese Rhetoric Reimagined*, edited by C. Jan Swearingen and LuMing Mao. *College Composition and Communication* 60, no. 4 (June 2009): W32–W121.

Young, Richard E., Alton L. Becker, and Kenneth L. Pike. *Rhetoric: Discovery and Change*. New York: Harcourt, 1970.

Zappan, James. "Francis Bacon." In *Encyclopedia of Rhetoric and Composition: Communication from Ancient Times to the Information Age*, edited by Theresa Enos, 61–63. New York: Routledge, 1996.

ABOUT THE AUTHOR

Lisa Blankenship is an assistant professor of English and writing director at Baruch College, City University of New York. Her research focuses on rhetorical ethics and engagement across marked social differences, both historically and in contemporary, digital contexts. She has published in *Present Tense: A Journal of Rhetoric in Society* and *Computers and Composition*.

INDEX

Aaim, Muhammad Madi Abu al-, *The Great Court of Ṣulḥ*, 37
Abel, Mary Hinman, 64–65
Abitol, David, 124–25
acting, surface and deep, 8–9
action, emotion and, 43–44
activism: Jane Addams', 61–62; Joyce Fernandes, 62–63; Justin Lee's, 84–100
Activist WPA: Changing Stories about Writing and Writers, The (Adler-Kassner), 108–9
ACT UP, 125
Addams, Jane, 11, 64, 121, 126; Columbian Exposition speech, 22, 61–62, 64–65, 66–68, 70–73, 135(n1); rhetorical style, 68–69, 94, 123–24
Adler-Kassner, Linda, 56–57, 93; *The Activist WPA*, 108–9
aesthetics, in Euro-American rhetoric, 45–47
affect, 6, 10, 34
African Americans, as domestic workers, 67
agency, 94–95
Age of Empathy, The (de Waal), 125–26
Ahmed, Sara, 34
American Grace: How Religion Unites and Divides Us (Putnam), 123
American Woman's Home, The (Beecher and Beecher Stowe), 71–72
Ames, Roger T., *Anticipating China*, 29, 31, 33
Analects (Confucius), 41–42
Anthony, Susan B., 65
Anticipating China: Thinking Through the Narratives of Chinese and Western Culture (Hall and Ames), 29, 31, 33
antigay rhetoric, 85
Arab-Islamic traditions, 29, 32, 35–37
argument(s), 138(n4); rhetoric as, 106–8; virtuous, 24–25

Aristotle, 30, 47–48, 106, 131(n6), 133(n36); *On Rhetoric*, 21, 27, 29, 38–40
"Ask a . . ." blog series, 84, 136(n1)
"Ask a Gay Christian" blog, 83, 89, 96–97, 98–99, 101
audience, 115; change and, 98–99; for composition, 104, 114; engagement of, 100–101; motives of, 92–94, 96–97, 101–2; and rhetoric, 21–22; in Rogerian rhetoric, 48–49
Augustine, 31
Available Means (Ritchie and Ronald), 55

Bacon, Francis, 43, 133(n47)
bargain-rhetoric, 50
Barna, George, 88
Baruch College (City University of New York), 11; composition classes at, 24, 103–4; first-year writing assignments at, 109–17; writing groups at, 117–19
Battiste, Marie, 29
BBC, Joyce Fernandes and, 23, 62–63
Bean, John C., *Writing Arguments*, 107
Becker, Alton, 48; *Rhetoric*, 49, 138(n9)
Beecher, Catharine Esther, *The American Woman's Home*, 71–72
being-with-others, 18, 29, 128
"Belated Industry, A" (Addams), 66, 69; on domestic workers, 70–73
Belenky, Mary Field, 138(n19); *Women's Ways of Knowing*, 56
Benhabib, Seyla, 134(n84); on public-private dichotomy, 58–59
Berthoff, Ann, 105
"Beyond Persuasion: A Proposal for an Invitational Rhetoric" (Foss and Griffin), 55
bian, 21, 32–33
Bishop, Wendy, 105

understanding, 48, 49, 118; Other, 57–58
unions, female workers', 66
utilitarianism, 58

Vetlesen, Arne Johan, personal as political, 59–60
Vischer, Robert, 26; *On the Optical Sense of Form*, 45–46
vulnerability, and change, 14, 98–99

Welty, Eudora, "Must the Novelist Crusade?," 3–4
Westboro Baptist Church, 124
What Diantha Did (Gilman), 65–66
"What I Learned at School" (Corder), 116
"When the First Voice You Hear Is Not Your Own" (Royster), 19
whites, evangelical Protestantism, 87
Windsor Supreme Court, marriage equality case, 24, 87
Wispé, Lauren, 6
women, 65, 121; in domestic service, 66–67, 69–73, 74, 75, 76–79; rhetorical form by, 54–55

Women's Congress, 61–62, 135(n2)
women's rights movement, 121
Women's Trade Union League, 66
Women's Ways of Knowing (Belenky et al.), 56
working conditions, 20, 63, 135(n10)
Working Women's Association of America Union, 66
World's Columbian Exposition, speeches at, 61, 64, 65, 135(n1)
World's Congress of Representative Women, 65, 66
writing, 118; conflict in, 107–8; digital classes, 116–17; pedagogy, 115–16; personal, 105–6, 110–15
Writing Arguments (Ramage, Bean, and Johnson), 107
writing groups, 117–18

Xunzi, 33

Yancey, Kathleen Blake, 15
Young, Richard, 48; *Rhetoric*, 49, 138(n9)

Zigong, 42